Enrollment Management

Enrollment Management

Successful Approaches with Dwindling Numbers

Edited by
Perry R. Rettig

ROWMAN & LITTLEFIELD
Lanham • Boulder • New York • London

Published by Rowman & Littlefield
An imprint of The Rowman & Littlefield Publishing Group, Inc.
4501 Forbes Boulevard, Suite 200, Lanham, Maryland 20706
www.rowman.com

6 Tinworth Street, London SE11 5AL, United Kingdom

Copyright © 2021 by Perry R. Rettig

All rights reserved. No part of this book may be reproduced in any form or by any electronic or mechanical means, including information storage and retrieval systems, without written permission from the publisher, except by a reviewer who may quote passages in a review.

British Library Cataloguing in Publication Information Available

Library of Congress Cataloging-in-Publication Data

Names: Rettig, Perry Richard, editor.
Title: Enrollment management : successful approaches with dwindling numbers / edited by Perry R. Rettig.
Description: Lanham : Rowman & Littlefield, [2021] | Includes bibliographical references.
Identifiers: LCCN 2021009858 (print) | LCCN 2021009859 (ebook) | ISBN 9781475860566 (cloth) | ISBN 9781475860573 (paperback) | ISBN 9781475860580 (epub)
Subjects: LCSH: College attendance—United States—Planning. | College students—Recruiting—United States. | Universities and colleges—United States—Admission. | Universities and colleges—United States—Administration.
Classification: LCC LC148.2 .E58 2021 (print) | LCC LC148.2 (ebook) | DDC 378.1/980973—dc23
LC record available at https://lccn.loc.gov/2021009858
LC ebook record available at https://lccn.loc.gov/2021009859

Enrollment Management is dedicated to those individuals and those teams working every day, most often in isolation, to bring success to our colleges and our students. The myriad challenges today seem insurmountable. We need to join their efforts by listening to them and becoming active participants. We need to engage, to be persistent in our support, and to break away from our mimetic isomorphism, or our blinded vision of our own experiences of the way things are. The old models of recruitment and retention may have worked in the past, but they are certainly obsolete now.

Finally, I dedicate this book to my mother and father—Maxine and Marwood Rettig. Indeed, they have been persistent in their support, engaged in my professional endeavors, and active listeners and participants. This modeling has developed the professional ethos necessary for creating and nurturing my approach to leadership and for my vision of higher education. It was my father who recited my favorite quote of Martin Luther:

"Here I stand; I can do no other."

Contents

Preface	ix
Acknowledgments	xix
Introduction	1

1 Finding and Analyzing the Data, Financial Aid, and the Registrar — 9
  Essay: Jody Anderson—Finding and Analyzing the Data — 10
  Essay: Lisa Danielson and Perry Rettig—The Enigmatic Office of the Registrar — 17
  Essay: Beatriz Contreras—Financial Aid from 30,000: A Retrospective View — 20
  Essay: David McMillian—Boots on the Ground — 27
  Notes — 31

2 Admissions, Recruiting, and Marketing — 33
  Essay: Cindy Peterson—The Undergraduate Admissions Life Cycle — 36
  Essay: Kathleen Carter—The World of Graduate Admissions — 42
  Coda—Perry Rettig — 53
  Notes — 54

3 Student Success and Retention — 57
  Introduction — 57
  Essay: Cat Wiles and Perry Rettig—The Student Retention Vortex — 59

	Essay: Jenni Walsh—Using High Impact Practices in Student Affairs	64
	Essay: Petra Roter—Student Affairs—The View from 30,000 Feet	68
	Notes	72
4	The Curricular and the Cocurricular Juxtaposition	75
	Essay: Emily Pettit, Kim Crawford, and Perry Rettig—Student Services, Residence Life, and Leadership	77
	Essay: Jim Peeples—Athletics and Leadership: Recruit with Relationships as the Focal Point	86
	Essay: Julia M. Schmitz and Melissa Tingle—High Impact Practices	93
	Coda—Rettig	101
	Notes	102
5	Strategic Enrollment Management and Planning: The SEM and SEP	105
	Essay: P. J. Woolston—The Science of Strategic Enrollment Planning	108
	Essay: Perry Rettig—The Art of Strategic Enrollment Planning	116
	Coda—Perry Rettig	124
	Notes	126
Bibliography		129
About the Author		133

Preface

We have all read the stories of college and university closures due to declining enrollments. They are more than stories; they are reality. Much of the country has already been experiencing plummeting high school graduation rates.[1] States that have yet to experience this phenomenon will not be spared. Doss Bowman gave a stark reality check: "The freefall of traditional college-age students is already having an impact on higher education and the competition for students will continue to increase and put pressure on universities to prove their value and retain their financial vitality."[2] Indeed, the need for new student recruitment and retention strategies is imperative.

The pressures on senior leadership and governing boards appear insurmountable. "Those providing leadership for colleges and universities in the United States are facing increasingly complex and unrelenting challenges that stretch their capacity to understand fully and to respond effectively to what the future may hold."[3] Shinn further stipulated, "Of the many external forces higher education must address, two in particular interact to create an urgent and compelling need for colleges and universities to engage in a systematic assessment of their enrollment/financial (i.e., net tuition) model and the effectiveness of their traditional teaching/learning paradigm."[4]

Senior Consultant with the American Association of Collegiate Registrars and Admissions Officers, Clayton Smith (and his colleagues) also noted, "Among the most common pressures are decreasing enrollments, decreasing funding, increasing costs, increasing diversity, changing expectations of learners, and changing expectations of employers."[5]

Government fiscal support for higher education has been declining for years. "[T]hey place a greater burden on colleges and universities to compete for enrollments, grants, and tuition dollars."[6] Jeffrey Selingo provided the data which supports what we already know: spending per student grew faster in the last decade than ever before—27 percent at private institutions and 42 percent at their public counterparts.[7] "According to the College Board, the average sticker price . . . at public institutions . . . has risen by more than 60% since the year 2000. At private colleges, the total price is . . . up nearly 40% over the same period."[8]

While costs to maintain colleges continue to rise, the burden is felt equally by families. Again, the College Board noted in a study, "More than 80% are concerned about the cost of higher education."[9] These rising costs accompanied with family inability to pay has forced universities to increase their Discount Rates each year resulting at times in decreasing Net Tuition Revenue.[10] According to Shinn, "Current revenue strategies that presume continued enrollment growth and untethered tuition discounting are unsustainable."[11]

American colleges and universities, both public and private, are experiencing a demographic shift like none they have seen in decades.[12] WICHE data indicates that an enrollment crisis has already hit the Northeast and Midwest regions of our nation, while the other regions will see significant enrollment declines by the middle of the decade.[13] Revenue streams continue to dry up, public support continues to diminish; the result is an increase in college closures.[14] The old model isn't working, but it never really did.

A cursory glance at declining high school enrollments might suggest difficult but manageable losses for institutions of higher learning. However, a deeper analysis indicates much more dire problems. Traditional white college-attending populations are showing double-digit declines. Any potentially mitigating differences are made up by near-term growth in underrepresented populations. Miller notes, Gen Z marks the last generation in U.S. history where a majority of the population is white . . . Gen Z is so diverse that we don't even recognize diversity."[15]

Three concerns quickly emerge from this insight. First, these underrepresented populations are less likely to matriculate onto college rolls.[16] Second, should they enroll, they are less likely to persist toward graduation.[17] Third, these same populations, however, earn roughly 60 percent total family income of their majority counterparts,[18] and are typically less prepared for college.

By the end of the decade, even these populations show a precipitous drop. The reason for the overall population decline? With the economic crisis—the Great Recession—in 2008–2009, families had fewer children.[19]

Despite these harrowing data sets, however, there is one population that is significantly robust at the present and shows continued growth into the future. Doss Bowman notes, "The majority of students enrolled in colleges and universities are older, nontraditional age."[20] Working adults are the most overlooked demographic in America, today. More focus on this expansive opportunity, later. For now, a description of the current traditional college-attending student is in order. Just who is Gen Z?

Each generation is inextricably shaped by its context and era. This fact is no less true for Gen Z—those young people born between roughly the years 1995 and 2010. These youth saw the international War on Terrorism, school shootings, their parents lose their jobs and finances in the Great Recession, racial disharmony, and are living through an international COVID-19 pandemic. Their parents have made decisions for them and have set goals for them. They have grown up with the ubiquitous nature of technology; they are the YouTube generation.

According to reports cited by Schwieger, "91% of teens studied have access to a smartphone, 69% have access to a tablet, and 90% watch YouTube daily."[21] Selingo noted these students "reflexively turn to YouTube for information . . . [and] many spend more time on their devices than they do in face-to-face encounters."[22]

Today's students are entrepreneurial, persistent, and self-sufficient. They like to find information on their own rather than turn to others for help.[23] These same attributes make them pragmatic and career focused, especially considering what happened to their parents. They want to know their degree holds value and is relevant and leads to a stable career. In fact, they believe the purpose of college is to get a career. Selingo explained, "[t]hey will look primarily for academic and co-curricular programs to develop their skills and prospects."[24]

Finances are always at the forefront of these students' minds. They have witnessed their parents' struggles through both the Great Recession and the COVID-19 pandemic. This has made them "concerned about their financial futures including the cost of college and accumulating student loan debt."[25] To which Selingo added, "They shop for a good value, appreciate price transparency, and want to estimate their return on investment."[26]

Writing for XYZ University in *HR Magazine,* then high school student Josh Miller described the dual nature of Gen Z students. He explained that they like to work independently, wish to be entrepreneurial, and are always "connected," but they lack, and therefore, "crave" human interaction.[27] All these compounding concerns just elucidated indicate Gen Z students are coming to today's campuses with more mental health issues and need various support services (eg. mental health, career services, tutoring), and they want them when they want them—instantaneously.[28]

As Gen Z students have a particular career focus and various needs from their professors and support staff, they hold similar expectations of their future bosses. Schwieger stipulated, "Gen Z respondents cited their most important characteristics associated with future employers to include: treating people with respect, ethical behavior, fair compensation and promotion across all employees, open and transparent communication, and wise business decision-making."[29]

Professor at the University of Illinois Springfield, Vickie Cook added to this list: this generation "values rewards that offer *more autonomy and freedom* [emphasis in original], such as flexible work hours, working from home, online and hybrid approaches to working and learning."[30]

Not only is Gen Z dissimilar than its preceding generation, today's workforce has different needs and expectations of them. Boards of Trustees and senior university leadership need to understand these workforce demands of today and of the future. The Association of American Colleges and Universities surveys CEOs and hiring managers to determine the priorities they are looking for from college graduates. "The top six priorities include: oral communication; teamwork skills with diverse groups; written communication; critical thinking and analytical reasoning; complex problem solving; and, information literacy."[31]

In similar fashion, The National Association of Colleges and Employers conducted a study of employers and found the top six required skills, in order, were: ability to work in a team; problem-solving skills; written communication skills; strong work ethic; verbal communication skills; and, leadership.[32] Terrel Rhodes cited additional research: "78% of business executives say it's very important that their workers possess critical thinking skills . . . 60% of hiring managers say they would be much more likely to hire recent graduates who have completed an internship . . . 78%

of executives prefer e-portfolios to express student academic achievements as opposed to transcripts alone."[33]

Finally, in the March/April 2020 Association of Governing Boards *Trusteeship* journal, Karen Doss Bowman was quoted:

> [Wheaton College President Dennis Hanno] believes Wheaton's efforts to provide practical academic programs that incorporate the strengths of a liberal arts approach has appealed to a broader base of prospective students . . . The programs help students develop the soft skills employers are looking for—critical thinking, written and oral communication, problem solving, and the ability to collaborate in a team setting—through practical experiences that require applying those qualities in a real-world setting.[34]

There remain reasons university and college leaders to be plausibly optimistic. In the near term, underrepresented populations, more particularly Hispanic and Asian, are showing potential for enrollment growth. There is an even larger group which has for the most part been untouched, and that is nontraditional students—those over twenty-five years of age. It should be noted that not all of these students need to attend college in order to complete a degree; many wish to seek smaller credentials. Still others have varying numbers of academic credits banked to transfer.

There are still other reasons for hope. "Not only is there greater demand for higher education among students of color, but also students from low-income backgrounds, those from rural communities, older adults, U.S. military veterans, and adults with full-time jobs."[35] Further, high school students whose parents have attended college are more likely to attend themselves. This population will increase by 7 percent by the end of the decade according to Nathan Grawe.[36]

Along with these encouraging data points, higher education leaders can develop numerous strategies to begin mitigating previously noted concerns. In fact, most of these strategies will likely make their institutions more resilient and even stronger than they have ever been before. At the same time, such strategies often need not be excessively expensive; gone are the days of extravagant amenities—Gen Z doesn't care for them.

Generally, such strategies should focus on both the recruitment and retention of students and can range from the curricular (programs and pedagogy) to the co-curricular. Focus will be on emerging student populations, as well as parents, alumni, and employers. Student support services, modest physical plant adjustments, and utilization of new technologies must be considered. New budgeting processes, data management, and financial aid support will benefit students and institutions alike. New community partnerships and student experiences will be essential. These will be covered in finer detail throughout this book and will be of particular focus in chapter 5.

The alternative, of course, is to attempt to maintain the status quo and continue with business as usual. Nathan Grawe told us how to brace for this strategy: "Perhaps, institutions need to prepare for significant staff and faculty reductions within the next 15 years and not simply redesign our recruitment and teaching strategies."[37] Conversely, we can break from our mimetic isomorphism—our vision of the only way we know how to do things—and create through a new lens of opportunity and collaboration.

NOTES

1. Nathan Grawe. *Demographics and the Demand for Higher Education.* Baltimore, MD: Johns Hopkins University Press. 2018.

   Grawe specifies the interstate migration from the Northeast and the Pacific to the South and to the West. He further stipulates "greater shares among Hispanic, Asian, and Southwest subgroups." (9)

   Grawe calculates college population potentialities based on the Higher Education Demand Index (HEDI). Demand for College = Probability of attendance X Number of Children.

2. Karen Doss Bowman. "Shifting Demographics." *Trusteeship:* Association of Governing Boards of Universities and Colleges. (March/April, 2020). 28(2): 21.

3. Larry Shinn. "No, It's Not Just the Enrollment Crisis—It's Also Time to Modify Our Learning Paradigm," *Trusteeship:* Association of Governing Boards of Universities and Colleges. (May/June 2020), 28(3), 20.

4. Ibid. 20.

5. Clayton Smith, Janet Hyde, Tina Falkner, and Christine Kerlin. "The Role of Organizational Change Management in Successful Strategic Enrollment Management Implementation," *Strategic Enrollment Management Quarterly, 8*(2): Summer 2020, 33.

6. Aaron Hanlon. "Higher Ed Is Not a Zero-Sum Game: Cutthroat Competition Is Not the Way Forward." *Chronicle of Higher Education.* June 19, 2020.

7. Jeffrey Selingo. "The New Generation of Students: How Colleges Can Recruit, Teach, and Serve Gen Z." Washington, DC: *The Chronicle of Higher Education.* 2018, 33.

8. Ibid. Selingo, 19. Selingo expanded on this problem: "Now many campuses are saddled with construction debt and deferred-maintenance backlogs. More generally,

institutions' expense growth is catching up to or even outpacing their revenue growth. A quarter of public colleges reported declining revenue . . . while the same proportion of private colleges ran operating deficits." (16)

Larry Shinn provided three sobering data points/critiques: "Even with an average 52.2 percent tuition discount rate for first-year students, only 34 percent of private colleges and universities poled met their enrollment targets in 2019. A 2019 survey found that 79 percent of colleges said they intend to increase their enrollment to make their budgets balance. Moody's expects 4 percent operating expense growth this coming year with 50 percent of public university and 40 percent of private colleges falling below 3 percent revenue growth—hence, Moody's 'negative' financial outlook for all of higher education." (21)

Ibid. Shinn.

9. Ibid. Cited in Selingo, 19. Selingo adds that families' incomes have stagnated qualifying many as Pell Grant recipients (42). Due to this phenomena, many of these families refuse or are reluctant to take on student loan debt (19).

Hamilton et al. further cited the College Board, "[t]he rate of increase in tuition and fees still exceeds inflation" (113). Hamilton, Laura, Josipa Roksa, and Kelly Nielsen, "Providing a 'Leg Up': Parental Involvement and Opportunity Hoarding in College," SAGE: American Sociological Association, 2018: 91(2). Journals. sagepub.com/home/soe.

10. NACUBO. "Before COVID-19, Private College Tuition Discount Rates Reached Record Highs," Washington, DC: National Association of College and University Business Officers. https://www.nacubo.org/Research/2020/NACUBO-Tuition-Discounting-Study. May 20, 2020.

11. Ibid. Shinn. 21.

12. Jeffrey Docking, *Crisis in Higher Education: A Plan to Save Small Liberal Arts Colleges in America* (East Lansing, MI: Michigan State University Press, 2015).

Docking is the President of Adrian College and has outlined four keys to successful enrollment growth: intentionally set enrollment targets for both academic programs and athletic teams; create new niche academic programs; introduce new athletic programs; and, create new Centers which promote the institution's mission.

13. WICHE: Western Interstate Commission for Higher Education (*Knocking at the College Door* 2016).

Additional and supporting data can be found at: U.S. Department of Education, Institute of Education Sciences, National Center for Education Statistics (*Digest of Education Statistics,* 2017).

14. Robert Zemsky, Susan Shaman, and Susan Campbell Baldridge, *The College Stress Test: Tracking Institutional Futures Across a Crowded Market* (Baltimore, MD: Johns Hopkins University Press, 2020).

15. Josh Miller. "10 Things You Need to Know about Gen Z." *HR Magazine.* SHRM.org, October 30, 2018. 10.

16. Ibid. Grawe. 24.

17. Laura Hamilton, Josipa Roksa, and Kelly Nielsen, "Providing a 'Leg up': Parental Involvement and Opportunity Hoarding in College," SAGE: American Sociological Association, 2018: 91(2), 114. Journals.sagepub.com/home/soe.

18. College Board, *Trends in College Pricing* www.collegeboard.org. 2018.

President of Albion College (MI) foretold these concerns: "Economic insecurity throughout the country compounds enrollment problems at many small private colleges because parents and students believe students won't find jobs that will enable them to pay off college debt." Jeffrey Docking, 2015, 9.

19. Ibid. Doss Bowman. Citing research by the Center for Disease Control (CDC), Doss Bowman noted, " . . . the total fertility rate in the United States has dropped by nearly 20 percent . . ." (22).

According to Grawe, the fertility rate has decrease 12% since 2007. Nathan Grawe. *Demographics and the Demand for Higher Education.* Baltimore, MD: Johns Hopkins University Press. 2018, 6.

To this end, Grawe adds, "While the birth dearth may increase the pace of decline slightly, there is no period of respite before contraction. In total, by 2032 WICHE foresees 15 percent fewer non-Hispanic white high school graduates than there are today." (17)

20. Ibid. Doss Bowman. 21.
21. Dan Schwieger and Christine Ladwig. "Reaching and Retaining the Next Generation: Adapting to the Expectations of Gen Z in the Classroom." *Information Systems Education Journal 16*(3). June 2018. 46.

Professor Vickie Cook added that this generation is connected all the time. Cook, Vickie. https://sites.google.com/a/uis.edu/colrs_cook/

22. Ibid. Selingo. 5, 9. "Knowledge is everywhere for these students. They are accustomed to finding answers instantaneously on Google while doing homework or sitting at the dinner table . . . they expect faster feedback from everyone, on everything." (9)
23. Ibid. Schwieger. 46.
24. Ibid. Selingo. 4.
25. Ibid. Schwieger. 48.
26. Ibid. Selingo. 4.
27. Ibid. Miller. 11.
28. Ibid. Selingo. 4. Selingo indicated there are "[r]ising reports of poor mental health" (9). To which he added two striking comments:

"Students are coming to us more like 14-year-olds and not 18-year-olds." (34)

"Gen Z is coming to college less seasoned than previous generations. Teenagers today tend not to go to the movies with friends, hang out at the mall, or spent time at friends' houses; most go out with their parents and communicate with their friends digitally." (37)

29. Ibid. Schwieger. 46.
30. Ibid. Cook. She continued: "Generation Z need *rewards that are changed frequently* [emphasis in original] to meet changing expectations and demands."
31. Hart Research Associates. "Key Findings from 2018 Employer Research." Washington, DC: *Fulfilling the American Dream: Liberal Education and the Future of Work*. American Association of Colleges and Universities. www.aacu.org/leap/public-opion-research.
32. Ibid. Schwieger. 49.

33. Terrel Rhodes. "The Changing Nature of Work and Careers," Washington, DC: Association of American Colleges & Universities, *Liberal Education 105*(3/4), Summer/Fall 2019, 8–10.

34. Ibid. Doss Bowman. 21–22.
35. Ibid. Doss Bowman. 23.
36. Ibid. Grawe. 55.
37. Ibid. Grawe. 19.

Acknowledgments

It is quite apparent this book would not be possible without the work of my fellow essayists. They were chosen because of their wealth of experience in higher education and their dedication to student success. I have learned a great deal from them, and it has been a privilege to work alongside them over these years.

I must also acknowledge the support and encouragement from those senior executive leaders and board members over the years who have been active listeners and participants in our teams' trials and tribulations. Without foresight and persistence, success would be fleeting. Finally, but of equal value, is the prescient vision and guidance of Tom Koerner. His instincts and leadership at Rowman & Littlefield are making a difference in the contemporary landscape of higher education.

Introduction

There are highly paid experts and consulting firms across the country willing to help you prepare for the requisite changes ahead. Interestingly, most of these experts no longer work directly in the field with the changing demographics and are not held to account like college practitioners with demands to increase recruitment and retention numbers. But real-life practitioner-experts exist. In fact, you know them; they work with you.

This book is a collection of wisdom and experiences from some of those very practitioner-experts. These are the people who are held accountable every day; they know the literature; they have the practical experience; they are wise; and they know what they're doing. These field experts are going to share with you the experiences they have lived and are living. Each will give you a lay of the land for their area. They will explain the unique endeavors they developed, implemented, and led. They will share their successes, as well as lessons learned—what they would do differently if they could do it all over again. And some will conclude by sharing with you things they would do now if they just had a small additional amount of resources (e.g., one more staff member, or $10,000 more in their budgets).

These former and current colleagues of mine will express the myriad complexities of enrollment management and the interconnections and collaborations necessary to make strategic enrollment planning work at the ground level. The domain of enrollment management is a very broad and comprehensive central aspect of every university in our nation. While it is complex and intricately woven within every other division across the university, a strategic and robust vision makes it all approachable and manageable. As most private colleges have an operating budget which relies in excess of 90 percent on student tuition and associated auxiliary revenues, effective enrollment management is essential and central to each institution's survival. This book traverses the landscape of a comprehensive approach to enrollment management. Five chapters will feature the varied components of a campus-wide model. While organizational structure will vary across universities, the general components will all share common features. In any case, collaborative efforts and effective communication and partnerships across divisions, units, and domains is critical.

My direction to these essayists was simple: the audience for this book consists of members of boards of trustees, university executive leadership, and those new to enrollment management leadership positions. With that said, these individuals make critical institutional decisions and are the primary leadership of the campus—what do you wish they understood about your area of responsibility in order to make wise decisions? Tell them what you wish they would know. Tell them of strategies that have worked for you, as well as things you would now do differently. Give them advice. And, finally, if you had a modest budget increase or could add one more staff member, what would you do—to take your work to the next level?

While these essays are stand-alone and distinctive briefs, the work of these individuals, for the most part, is not done in isolation but rather in a great deal of complex and comprehensive interaction—often on a daily basis. So, while there are distinctive chapters in this book, the work of these individuals and the units they lead is not in any way isolated. The nature of their jobs and the tasks they must complete requires fully integrative and collaborative team approaches. Successful enrollment management simply can't be done otherwise.

In chapter 1, we begin with data. Our institutions are dripping with data; it is ubiquitous, but often we don't know where it is, how to get to it, or how to analyze it. Jody Anderson writes an essay describing this all too common dilemma and how he has tackled it. Anderson is the director of Institutional Research at Piedmont University and had previously served as associate director of Financial Aid. Anderson has been able to reimagine data analytics at the university and pull together disparate data sets which have been instrumental in predictive analytics as well as financial aid modeling for the institution.

Three additional essays are featured in chapter 1. Director emerita of Financial Aid at the University of Wisconsin Oshkosh, Beatriz Contreras, gives a 30,000-foot view and historical perspective of financial aid. Her forty years of experience gave her wisdom and unparalleled experience in the field. David McMillion explains the ruminations of the Financial Aid Office and its myriad federal and state bureaucratic mandates—all in terms for the lay reader. McMillion had served as director of Financial Aid at Piedmont College before moving to the position of associate director of Financial Aid at the University of North Georgia. Further, he co-chaired the Retention Vortex efforts across the campus.

Lisa Danielson has over two decades experience as registrar and thirty-five years in higher education. This office is often considered enigmatic to those outside the academy. Lisa will provide a very approachable discussion of the responsibilities of this office and how it interfaces with other offices across the campus. Danielson is the registrar at the University of Wisconsin Oshkosh. She brings a wealth of experience to the enrollment process from both recruitment and retention perspectives. The Office of Veteran Affairs also reports to Ms. Danielson.

Chapter 2 is devoted to the offices of Undergraduate and Graduate Admissions—those individuals responsible for recruiting and marketing. These offices are often the face of the university and the first formal interaction for prospective students. The focus of different types of colleges and universities has a significant impact on these offices. For example, technical colleges, liberal arts colleges, comprehensive universities, and research universities each have particular missions which draw particular types of students who in turn need different recruiting strategies.

The first essay in chapter 2 is penned by Cindy Peterson. She will explain both the inward and outward facing aspects of this essential office. Admissions staff members are considered the "road warriors" of any university, yet their impact on student retention is undeniable. Peterson is the associate vice president for Undergraduate Admissions at Piedmont University. From her collaborative efforts with the Retention Vortex, she has created a parallel admissions vortex. Cindy has played a critical role in Piedmont's enrollment management strategies over the years, as well as strategic enrollment planning initiatives.

Graduate admissions is impacted by the university mission perhaps more than any other unit within enrollment management. For example, R1 institutions have very different processes for admittance than do liberal arts colleges. Chapter 2 is concluded by Kathleen Carter. Carter is associate vice president for Graduate Enrollment Management at Piedmont University. She has led efforts to increase enrollments for both on-campus, as well as off-campus cohort and online programs for twenty-one years. Her experience encompasses masters, specialist, and doctoral degrees. Carter has a breadth of home-grown experience in trending analytics.

Chapter 3 turns to student success and retention. While the previous chapter focused on landing new enrollments and the right mix of students, this chapter focuses on putting in place programs, protocols, and structures to support student retention and enable matriculated students to persist toward graduation. Of all the efforts colleges have implemented to leverage student revenue, student retention has received the least attention, yet it is likely to have the greatest impact.

Three essays make up the triumvirate of chapter 3. Cat Wiles is the administrative assistant to the vice president for Enrollment Management and Student Affairs at Piedmont University. Wiles serves as co-chair of the Retention Vortex and is the retention software manager for the university. Operationally speaking, she serves as the liaison between faculty and the enrollment management staff. In this essay, Wiles outlines the university's Retention Vortex and its enterprise retention software process. Dr. Perry Rettig contributes to this essay describing Piedmont University's student success offices and initiatives.

Jenni Walsh is former executive director of the Wisconsin Campus Compact at the University of Wisconsin-Extension, and student services director and academic advisor at the University of Wisconsin Platteville-Baraboo Sauk County. Walsh's experiential background encompasses student recruitment, retention, transfer, at-risk, and veteran student populations. Walsh's essay explicates the myriad student services necessary to meet the needs of Gen Z and underrepresented student populations. She brings eighteen years of higher education experience to her work.

Dr. Petra Roter is former vice chancellor of Student Affairs at the University of Wisconsin Oshkosh. With these responsibilities, she oversaw Admissions, Financial Aid, Residence Life, Dean of Students, Career Services, Intercollegiate Athletics, Dining Services, Health Center, Counseling Center, EAP, University Police, and more. In her thirty-five year career in higher education, Roter also served as interim vice president for Academic Affairs and Student Affairs at the University of Wisconsin System, and then as senior special assistant to the vice president. Roter describes an expansive view of student support services at the same time describing the philosophy behind programming and policy.

Chapter 4 focuses on Student Life and the interface with Academic Affairs. Gone are the days of isolating curricular and co-curricular silos in higher education. Today's institutions must have at their core a dynamic, interconnected community. Our students expect this, and our employers demand it. Kim Crawford and Emily Pettit pen the first essay in this chapter by describing student life outside the classroom and the support systems necessary to help our students.

Crawford is dean of Student Life and Leadership at Piedmont University. Dr. Crawford oversees the areas of: Residence Life, Orientation, Greek Life, Student Organizations, and Student Recreation and Wellness. She also leads campus initiatives for Student Leadership. She is a member of the campus Strategic Planning Leadership Team. Pettit is the Associate Vice President for Student Success at Piedmont. The offices which report to her include: Tutoring Services. Career Services, Counseling Services, Experiential Learning, and the Office of Accessibility Resources and Services.

Jim Peeples is the director of Athletics at Piedmont University and former head baseball coach. Peeples has played a unique role straddling both recruitment and retention efforts at the university. He has been an integral leader for both strategic enrollment planning, as well as overall strategic planning at Piedmont and is also a member of the Strategic Planning Leadership Team. His essay describes his experiences at several DIII institutions and how strategic program growth is both attainable and sustainable in today's changing environment.

Dr. Julia Schmitz and Dr. Melissa Tingle collaborate in an essay showing how their institution took robust national student success research—in the academic domain—and implemented it at the local level. Schmitz is a professor of Biology and Coordinator of the Quality Enhancement Program (QEP) at Piedmont University. She has served as QEP coordinator since its inception. The QEP focuses on high impact practices (HIPs), most notably: undergraduate research, global study/ travel away, and leadership. Tingle is a professor of Mass Communication at Piedmont University and QEP Fellow.

Tingle's Fellow responsibilities focus primarily on data analytics and assessment. She, along with Schmitz, also is responsible for coordinating Scholarship Days for undergraduate research at the university. These HIPs have proven to increase student retention.

Chapter 5 concludes this book by focusing on strategic enrollment planning (SEP). Dr. P. J. Woolston and Dr. Perry Rettig take turns elaborating on these critical planning efforts. Woolston begins with describing conceptual notions to SEP and gives the 30,000-foot view of planning efforts. Woolston is the vice president for Enrollment Management and Admissions at the University of Texas Permian Basin. He also serves as associate consultant for Ruffalo Noel-Levitz. Woolston is a national expert in enrollment management planning and financial modeling. He has served in senior-level positions at institutions across the nation and has consulted for numerous colleges and universities.

Rettig is vice president for Enrollment Management and Student Affairs at Piedmont University and also professor of Educational Administration and Leadership. While at Piedmont, Rettig has also served as vice president for Academic Affairs and vice president at the Athens Campus. In addition, he has served as interim dean of the School of Nursing & Health Sciences and interim dean of the School of Education. In his concluding essay, Rettig details actual SEP efforts he led at the university over the past three years. In other words, he explicates the pragmatic approach previously outlined in Woolston's essay.

The work of Rettig and his colleagues has been impactful. In three years, the institutional retention rate increased from 62 percent to 66 percent to 77 percent. Resident student populations have grown from 500 to 750 students in seven years. Such data indicate a miraculous turnaround. It could not be accomplished by one person or by happenstance. It has taken a team approach of dedicated faculty, staff, and senior leadership to make a concerted and deliberative effort of planning and action.

*It must be noted that Piedmont University moved from its status as Piedmont College in spring 2021. This explains the institution's name differentiation in several of the contributing author's descriptions above and in their later essays.

The task at hand is difficult and demanding, but it can be done. In fact, it is already being done, and successfully. It requires collaborations within the campus community, as well as across the external communities in which campuses find themselves. This is what gives me hope. I serve on two different chambers of commerce, and I interact with community leaders on a near daily basis. Our fellow community members love our college students. They want to be involved in developing the skills and talents of their emerging workforce. They want to hire these new alumni; they desperately want to be involved. This is our opportunity, our hope for success. They are ready to share if we are willing to listen and to engage.

This book is designed to be a quick read for the lay leader of today's colleges and universities. It will not be filled with esoteric literature, nor philosophical debates. Nor will it get lost in the weeds of minutia encompassed in the daily toils of the practitioner-expert. It will serve as a primer, and a how-to book. Moreover, it will describe what your institution can do tomorrow. Enjoy this opportunity to get to know and learn from my former and present colleagues. Their life experiences are matched by their eclectic approaches to writing these enlightening essays. Your read will be worth your time, I promise.

Chapter 1

Finding and Analyzing the Data, Financial Aid, and the Registrar

Whether you are a board member or a senior-level administrator on campus, you are well aware that data plays a critical and central role in your decision-making. Many institutions of higher learning have hired the services of outside companies to create elaborate data bases and tools for extracting their own data and for report writing. These efforts have proven their worth, yet at the same time they may not always be warranted. In other words, your institution already has the data, and you may already have the staff who can manipulate the data bases, provide the data analysis, and do the necessary reporting.

The offices of Institutional Research, Registrar, and Financial Aid are central repositories of such data. While other offices (e.g., Administrative Services, Institutional Effectiveness, Administrative Technology, Strategic Planning, and Admissions) also work with these and other data sets, these three offices are preeminent. "Managing enrollment expectations for institutional stakeholders requires effective communication, leadership, and the sharing of data with effective context."[1]

Most universities have created a cabinet-level Office of Enrollment Management which oversees all recruitment and retention efforts including data management. This office is able to manipulate data sets through pivot tables, create various scenarios, and disaggregate data for nuanced dialogue. Chancellor Dan Greenstein of the Pennsylvania State System explained, "[The assessment] disaggregates data by student group, such as by income, race, and ethnicity, so we are able deliberately to target and track progress elimination of attainment gaps."[2] Because of the unique types of data sets and the very unique nature of enrollment management, the language of these offices is often very foreign to those individuals who do not live in the field. Add to the mix federal and state reporting mandates, accreditation demands, and national databases (e.g., Integrated Postsecondary Education Data System [IPEDS], and the National Student Clearinghouse). It gets overwhelming to make sense of it all.

Pope and Davies further explain that there is a difference between data, information, and insights.[3] Consider data at the bottom of a pyramid—just raw numbers in isolation. Information is the data connected with context in an understandable fashion. Insights are explanations answering questions of so what and now what? So what does this tell us? Now what do we do as a result?

The essays to follow will help the reader navigate these foreign waters and define the terminology these offices toss out like candy at a parade. It has been said that second only to the armed forces, higher education uses more acronyms than any other organization or agency. There is both a special science and an art to enrollment management. Jody Anderson, Lisa Danielson, Beatriz Contreras, and David McMillion will be your guides helping you understand both this science and art. With roughly three-quarters of a century of experience between them, they will explain what a Registrar does, what the financial aid office is able to do, and the overall data abilities of the Office of Institutional Research.

ESSAY: JODY ANDERSON—FINDING AND ANALYZING THE DATA

Higher education in an information age places a particular importance on the collection, maintenance, and analysis of data. Decisions made by stakeholders at every level of an institution rely on the availability of accurate data from a multitude of sources. Information is collected, housed, and reported from many different offices on the college campus. An institution that values data will commit resources to support those responsible for its collection, maintenance, and reporting.

"Data-driven decision-making" is a phrase that has become pervasive in higher education administration during the past two decades much to the delight of the chart and spreadsheet loving "geeks" among us that tend to be drawn to the areas of institutional research (IR) and effectiveness (IE). Studies from the business world have shown greater efficiency from those who have adopted the data-driven approach.[4]

Those of us working in the IE and IR offices, along with many other offices working with large amounts of data on a daily basis, do not find this surprising. We may take pride in knowing that the stakeholders on our campuses value the work that we are doing to manage and present these data for use in the decision-making process. On the other hand, we may be frustrated when decisions don't seem to account for the data.

Perhaps the most important skill for stakeholders to develop in regard to the use of data in the decision-making process is the ability to ask the right question. Albert Einstein is attributed with saying, "If I had an hour to solve a problem and my life depended on it, I would use the first 55 minutes determining the proper question to ask, for once I know the proper question, I could solve the problem in less than five minutes."[5]

How do we ask the right questions when it comes to institutional data in our decision-making process? Provide specificity where possible when framing the request. While more data may be better, some parameters are necessary in every project. For example, suppose we are discussing graduation rates. We could ask for data on graduation rates. However, we might get more helpful results if we ask for graduation rates over the past ten years for students at our institution as compared to other schools in our athletic conference. Establishing these parameters when we ask the question will allow for more focused analysis to help in our decision making.

Another important and seemingly converse factor in asking the right question is to give the analyst a glimpse of the big picture. No one person can be expected to know all of an institution's data well enough to be able to ask the right question every time. However, individuals do exist throughout the institution that can help to frame those questions and to provide the answers. The more these data stewards understand about the reason for a request, the more they will be able to help us define the problem.

In addition to asking good questions, stakeholders play an important role in supporting the processes of data gathering and analysis. Administrators can support the process by ensuring that adequate resources are available to those responsible for maintaining and reporting data. They can set reasonable expectations when defining the scope and timetable of a project. Perhaps most importantly, they can provide constructive feedback throughout the process to help improve the quality and focus of the data analysis.

We have all heard the saying, "There are three kinds of lies: lies, damned lies, and statistics."[6] If we are to embrace the use of data in our decision-making processes, we must be open to allowing the data to have a true influence. The principle of confirmation bias tells us that if we approach a problem with the objective of finding data to support a decision we've already made, we are likely to find data that will support our decision. We get blue car syndrome. We buy a blue car, and all of a sudden all we see on the road is blue cars. Instead, we need focus our energy on defining the problem so that we can ask the right questions and allow the data to help us form the best solution.

Institutions of higher learning of every size have an abundance of data coursing through the system. Relevant information is generated from many sources, both internal and external to the institution, and it changes and accumulates constantly. Multiple methods and systems will exist within most institutions to gather and organize this ocean of data.

In colleges and universities, the Student Information System (SIS) is perhaps the largest and most important repository of information. In the grand scheme of higher education, most of us are not that far removed from paper files kept in multiple offices around campus for every student with little ability to cross reference between offices. Many of us still have stacks of boxes tucked away in dusty vaults somewhere on campus housing vital student information from past decades.

In the latter half of the twentieth century we began to move from paper to digital formats housed in homegrown databases, or what we now call "legacy systems." These first implementations of SIS represented a great leap forward in the ability of campuses to gather, organize, and access data. However, over time legacy systems tend to become outdated, unable to interact with other modern data sources, or too costly to maintain.[7]

While legacy systems are not necessarily a thing of the past, many institutions have adopted new models through Software-as-a-Service systems. Industry leaders like Ellucian, Salesforce, and PeopleSoft partner with institutions of higher learning to provide a regularly updated SIS—for a price. A modern SIS seeks to provide a good user interface, a stable environment, ease of access to data, and a high level of data security.

Institutions should include data collection and management in planning for the future. Whether this takes the form of upgrades to an aging legacy system, or a transition to an outside provider, resources will be required. A change from a legacy SIS, or even a transition from one provider to another, may take years of work from multiple offices across a campus.

The SIS is an important repository of data for every campus, but it is likely only one piece of a larger puzzle. Various offices on campus may maintain separate databases which may communicate with the SIS. Others may keep vast amounts of information in spreadsheets that are only accessible within a particular office. There are almost certainly paper files on campus containing data that doesn't make it into the SIS. All of these internal sources of data are important to the institution.

The Integrated Postsecondary Education Data System (IPEDS) is perhaps the largest and most important external repository of data in U.S. higher education. IPEDS is a group of surveys submitted each year by every postsecondary institution that participates in federal student aid programs. The completion of IPEDS surveys is typically the primary responsibility of the Institutional Research office but requires coordination of many offices across campus.

Established by the Higher Education Act of 1965, IPEDS collects data on a large cross section of the postsecondary landscape. As of 2020, the collection consisted of sixteen individual surveys spread out between four collection periods. Each of these surveys may require dozens of hours of data collection and review and must be completed each year. More than 7,500 institutions provide data through IPEDS, ranging from size of the incoming freshman class to the holdings in the library.[8]

The National Center for Education Statistics (NCES) makes all data collected through IPEDS available to the public. The NCES website[9] provides multiple tools for data analysis. The IPEDS Data Feedback Report provides an annual summary of each school's data compared against a preestablished group of peer institutions. The report can also be generated on demand with custom variables and comparison groups. The ability to obtain benchmarking data from any subset of participants is a valuable tool for institutions of higher education interested in data-driven decision-making.

Our small, private, liberal arts college has a historical mission of educating students from diverse socioeconomic backgrounds. A number of years ago, analysis of IPEDS data from peer institutions showed that, as expected, we were attracting a relatively large number of higher need and first-generation students. The data also showed that students in these populations tend to retain and graduate at lower rates. With this information in hand, we began to focus resources on supporting these populations and are beginning to see a positive impact on retention rates.

The reporting of institutional data to external agencies impacts the reputation of the institution. NCES provides IPEDS data designed for student/parent consumption through the College Navigator website.[10] The site allows the student to search for a particular college, or to navigate through a list of schools based on interest.

A number of entities offer rankings lists based on IPEDS data.[11] Others publish lists based on their own proprietary surveys which institutions complete voluntarily.[12] Lists are published based on a range of factors from affordability to best "party schools."[13] These rankings can provide fodder for our marketing departments when they are positive, but it is important to understand that the data does influence public perception.

A post-secondary institution may partner with multiple organizations for the collection, analysis, and reporting of data. Public colleges and universities likely have resources available through the state in which they operate along with additional reporting responsibilities at the state level. Private schools may participate in organizations like the Georgia Independent College Association (GICA), which collects data from member institutions and provides analysis in return.

Much like the SISs discussed earlier, the outsourcing of data analysis and support in higher education has become and industry unto itself. Companies like Emsi[14] combine education data with labor market data to help shape decisions around academic programming. Hanover Research[15] provides insights through consultation on topics ranging from enrollment management to marketing. Ruffalo Noel Levitz[16] offers tools to assist institutions from student recruitment to post graduation.

In addition to the management of the sizable amounts of passive data that exist within every institution of higher learning, most institutional researchers are also responsible for the active collection of data through survey administrations. Academic course evaluations are the largest and most frequent of these measures. Schools may take inventory of student, alumni, parent, and other stakeholder satisfaction on a regular basis. IR offices may also be asked to develop custom inquiries to faculty, staff, and other external entities. Survey administrations require investment of time and capital, but they can provide valuable input for decision making.

In recent years our college made an investment in an external tool to replace our in-house student satisfaction inventory. While the new instrument covered much of the same ground as our previous survey, we saw an immediate increase in student participation due to the more accessible format. Such externally driven surveys also help an institution to see how it rates compares to its competitors. A more robust survey and response will continue to provide valuable insight into student perception for our ongoing strategic planning process.

Institutional researchers need an expansive skill set to manage all of these data. Larger institutions may have specialty roles within the IR office which allow those who are happy to remain behind the scenes to remain hidden away doing analysis while those who prefer to be in front of a crowd are tasked with communicating that analysis to stakeholders. Smaller schools may rely on a single individual to write queries in the morning and make presentations to the board in the afternoon.

Regardless of the size of the enterprise a passion for data is beneficial for anyone working in the field. As in most areas of higher education, data science in continuously changing and advancing. Institutional researchers must have a willingness to continue to learn throughout their careers. Professional organizations like the Association for Institutional Research[17] provide continuing education in the field.

Stakeholders can help to support data processes by ensuring that the offices involved in data management have the resources needed to remain effective. Continuing education can be difficult if there is no room for it in the departmental budget. Researchers need funding to be able to participate in professional conferences. Offices need to be staffed at a level that allows some room for curiosity and creativity.

An effective Office of Institutional Research will work closely with area experts in offices throughout campus. The Admissions office is responsible for information about applicants and newly admitted students and may have valuable prospect data that is not tracked anywhere else. On our campus, IR works with Admissions to analyze student choice—why students are choosing our school and where they go when they don't. We also work together to evaluate how current student satisfaction might relate to future enrollments.

The Office of Financial Aid is responsible for some of the richest, and most protected, data available in higher education. Financial aid has multiple reporting requirements. Some of these, like IPEDS, may be coordinated through Institutional Research, while others may be handled within the Financial Aid office. At our institution, IR works with Financial Aid to analyze discount rates, to provide financial demographics to many reporting areas, and to relate student and alumni satisfaction to the financial aid process.

The Office of the Registrar is responsible for enrollment and academic data. IR works with the Registrar to track retention and graduation rates and to analyze academic factors which may influence those rates. The Registrar has one of the greatest burdens on campus in database integrity due to the sheer volume of data that passes through this office. IR depends on the Registrar to provide data for multiple components of IPEDS, many external surveys, and the course and enrollment information required to administer course evaluations.

Perhaps the offices with the most student contact on campus are Student Services, Student Affairs, and Athletics. These offices maintain data ranging from student housing to disability services. IR works closely with Student Services and Student Affairs to collect student satisfaction information and to share the results with the student body. Athletics and IR work together to report data to their governing body (the National Collegiate Athletic Association in our case) and to analyze patterns in student athlete enrollment.

On most campuses the Alumni office is responsible for an extensive amount of data. At our institution, IR collaborates with the Office of Institutional Advancement to survey our alumni on a regular basis. We have also partnered with a third-party to help analyze some of our alumni information for use in recruiting and academic program analysis.

These offices may exist under different names and share responsibilities differently on various college campuses. Institutional Research may be involved to a greater or lesser extent from school to school. The commonality is that the data exists, and that need to properly maintain it is imperative. The aforementioned need for financial resources and proper staffing in the IR office applies across every office in the institution if data integrity is to be protected.

The accessibility of reliable data will only increase in importance as we move further into this information age. Stakeholders at every level depend on accurate reporting to support the decision-making process. Institutions must commit appropriate resources in funding and staffing to the collection, maintenance, and analysis of data in every office on campus.

ESSAY: LISA DANIELSON AND PERRY RETTIG—THE ENIGMATIC OFFICE OF THE REGISTRAR

Of all the offices on a college campus, the Registrar is probably the most enigmatic. With a diverse array of responsibilities, the Registrar is hard to define because responsibilities differ across institutions. These responsibilities and scope of influence reach nearly every division across the campus, whether it be undergraduate or graduate, or face-to-face or online. Other than the Office of Financial Aid, this unit is likely the most regulated and formulaic following policies stipulated by the college, accrediting bodies, the state, and the federal government with privacy laws and records requests.

The most important duty of the Registrar is protecting the university's academic integrity. Almost every responsibility that pertains to the Registrar deals with that primary duty. Managing federal, state, and system policies while working collaboratively with faculty and staff on university policy make the Registrar's staff policy experts and data protectors for the campus. Further, this is the one office that touches each student's life from admissions to matriculation, and from graduation through alumni.

One of the most obvious responsibilities of Registrar's office is class registration for students. Registration can include building courses within a SIS, assisting departments/colleges with course array, adhering to registration policies and processes as dictated by the campus, course prerequisites, time conflicts, adding/dropping/withdrawing, registration appeals—the list is endless.

As most campuses know, the registration process is critical with enabling students a seamless, efficient, and positive experience. Monitoring registration numbers, and cycles within changing economic highs and lows, the Registrar is often tapped for trend analysis and assistance with enrollment management. In addition, the Registrar's office is most often tasked with running the early alert system which alerts faculty and staff if a student is struggling in classes, often before midterm grades are due. This allows support systems and advising to intervene before problems become too difficult for a student to overcome.

Transcripts and grade management is another obvious duty held by the Registrar. Encoding grading policies and procedures into the SIS while upholding data integrity and secure data transfer is crucial. The university transcript serves as the official document of the university and the official academic record for the student. It is imperative that this document is accurate, easy to read, and securely protected within the Registrar's office.

While some students may still want hard copy documents, the transcript has evolved to an electronic format and distribution. This creates a more efficient transmission of record to employers, other universities, and students. It is imperative that electronic records are held to the same security and protection.

Many Registrars are involved with transfer credit evaluation and test credit transcription. Understanding the need for credits to "count" for an incoming transfer student often times is the dealmaker or deal-breaker for a student. Knowing how a credit transfers and how it counts in degree progression is important for students, so making sure credit evaluation is correct and up to date is important. Some Registrars house the transfer student coordinator position so that highly individualized attention can be given to the transfer student. With more transfer and nontraditional students going back to school, this workload is increasing dramatically.

Degree audits, degree conferral, and graduation are also main responsibilities with the Registrar's office. Encoding of the degree audit involves department-approved curriculum, college degree requirements, and university policies and requirements. Assisting students with the navigation of their degree audit and working with students and faculty on curricular modifications is a daily process.

Graduation is a key time at the university and one of the most enjoyable responsibilities of the Registrar. Verifying that students have completed all degree requirements and assisting with the commencement ceremony happening after each semester. Universities differ on where commencement duties reside, but the Registrar maintains the official graduation list. They also report degree information and other reporting mandates to state and federal educational agencies, as well as institutional research for the campus. Diploma creation, whether internal or outsourced, is usually managed by the Registrar.

Registrar offices may also manage academic standing (probation/suspension). Notifying students of their academic standing and monitoring student appeals occurs after every semester. Registrars often times manage the appeal process with the academic colleges and departments. Academic standing is then reflected on the student transcript.

Registrars may also house the university Veteran Affairs benefits and resource centers. Military benefits are mandated by both federal and state agencies. So, we make sure the appropriate benefit is awarded and weekly reports are prepared for these agencies. In addition, we also contact veterans and family members about the benefits they receive. Registrars work with veterans and their families on campus support networks, deployment policies, veteran clubs, and so much more.

Registrars maintain the graduate and undergraduate catalogs and bulletins that house university, college, and department policies and degree requirements. This work is directly coordinated with Academic Affairs. The Registrar serves as the official student record custodian for academic records, and the office ensures the institution complies with all accreditation and governmental regulations for student privacy and securing student data. The Registrar's office works directly with the Office of Institutional Research on data collection, analysis, and reporting—IPEDS data is a prime example.

Further, the Registrar responds to academic and other department queries regarding enrollment data, course information, graduation and retention rates, and so on. Faculty seek policy advice from the Registrar for curriculum development and changes. Most often, the Registrar's office is responsible for oversight of federal FERPA regulations. FERPA is the Family Educational Rights and Privacy Act, which protects student records.

Enrollment management is an institution-wide responsibility, and the Registrar's office plays a critical role, both in terms of recruitment and retention. By creating policies and processes to be seamless, the campus community can do their work efficiently and accurately, all in a coordinated effort. This office usually reports to either Academic Affairs or to Enrollment Management, but the responsibilities clearly overlap both divisions.

A Vice President for Enrollment Management will likely interface with the Registrar's office on a nearly daily basis. During "registration season" each semester, the VPEM will want to know which students are not registering for the upcoming semester in order to mitigate obstacles and to assist students to register. Point-in-time comparisons of registrations to previous semesters is critical for planning and budgeting purposes for the institution.

The Registrar's office also analyzes data to determine if particular courses, or course sequences, cause bottlenecks to student progress toward graduation. For example, it may be found that a particular Biology course or sequence has the highest rate of withdrawals and failures. If this is the case, the institution can provide additional resources to support students in these courses (e.g., tutoring or supplemental instruction), or work with the faculty to assist them to better help students.

The Office of the Registrar is perhaps the one university entity most reliant on technology. Because of the vast data repositories, demands for data integrity and security, and requirements for data analysis and reporting, constant upgrades and professional development are mandatory. The University of Wisconsin Oshkosh is no different. The Registrar's office has made significant upgrades to its degree audit which better serves students and their advisors.

With additional funds, this office at UW Oshkosh could increase operational efficiencies for its new online secure format for information flow, forms, and processes. Such software upgrades may be expensive, but they create greater efficiencies within the office allowing better flexibility and service to faculty, staff, and students.

Again, the work of the Registrar and staff is heavily regulated and central to most functions of academic affairs and student affairs. Without collaboration, the system would collapse on itself and students would suffer. In a very real sense, these collaborations are partnerships with professional staff, faculty, and students; the work starts when a student matriculates, goes through their entire academic career through graduation, and certainly beyond as they become alumni.

ESSAY: BEATRIZ CONTRERAS—FINANCIAL AID FROM 30,000: A RETROSPECTIVE VIEW

This essay takes a retrospective view of the role of the Financial Aid office in Higher Education. It is the retrospective view sitting in the chair of a financial aid professional—a view that sees "the forest" as well as "the trees."

The Financial Aid office has existed in one form or another for the past seventy-six years or so, taking significant impetus with the establishment of the Servicemen Readjustment Act of 1944, which we know as the GI Bill. This law sought to assist veterans returning at the end of WW II. Educational benefits were part of this bill.

The next impetus happened with the enactment of the Higher Education Act (HEA) of 1965. This law expanded the access of federal funds to colleges and universities. It also redefined the term "financial assistance." The specific provisions of this law that cover financial assistance for students are covered under Title IV of the Higher Education Act of 1965. Title IV provided federal funding for scholarships, low interest student loans, work-study programs, and need-based grants.

The Higher Education Amendments of 1972 authorized the Basic Educational Opportunity Grant (BEOG) and the Supplemental Educational Opportunity Grant (SEOG). These need-based grants were created with the intention of offering aid to students based on financial need. The BEOG became what we now know as the Pell Grant, renamed after Senator Claiborne Pell. The result was the concept of financial aid packaging/awarding, with the Pell Grant serving as the base of the package and other federal, state, and institutional aid awarded up to the amount of a student's need.

Since 1972, every five or six years, Congress undertakes a process called Reauthorization. It is at this time that the federal student financial assistance programs are reviewed, continued or discontinued, and funding limits are set. The HEA included provisions that defined financial need and how to calculate this need. The BEOG, later renamed the Pell Grant, had its own need calculation formula embedded in the application process.

Financial Aid offices were authorized to calculate a student's financial need based on specific formulas. This is the beginning of what came to be known as "needs analysis." The concept is to look at the student and the family and determine an amount that the family would be expected to contribute toward the cost of education. This analysis needed to be consistent among all applicants and provide a fair assessment of the family's financial ability to contribute.

In the years from 1965 until 1986, there were several companies that provided this service to students and Financial Aid offices. The most important were the College Scholarship Service (CSS) and the American College Testing (ACT). Families completed either of these forms every year. The "needs analysis" report that was generated would be sent to the school or schools listed on the CSS or ACT Financial Aid Form (FAF). This was a yearly process, and each company charged a fee to process their form and send the needs analysis report to the school or schools listed on the form.

Families were therefore paying a fee in order to be considered for financial aid. This model served private institutions well because the form could calculate a needs analysis that helped these institutions award "institutional financial aid." These institutions could award their scholarships and other institutional aid using the calculated need from the CSS or ACT forms. Institutions could set their priority application date which helped them with early admissions and financial aid decisions. This was the basic concept of what we now call "Enrollment Management."

State colleges and universities also used the needs analysis calculations generated by the CSS and ACT. Enrollment management looked somewhat different at these institutions, because the foundation of the majority of the financial aid awards was not institutional aid but federal and state aid. The student profile was also different. Priority deadlines were helpful in managing early admissions decisions but that was not usual when the volume of applications was received.

The 1986 HEA Reauthorization decided that students should not have to pay to file a needs analysis form. The thinking was that families were paying in order to be considered for the free, need-based federal financial aid programs. It was determined that there would be a free form that students could use in order to apply for the federal financial aid programs. This form was simply called the common FAF and it used a uniform needs analysis that was called "Congressional Methodology."

This new methodology unified and simplified the various needs analysis systems that were in use across the country, and it introduced specific formulas to calculate what was called the "Expected Family Contribution" (EFC). The calculation for eligibility for the Pell Grant retained its own formula until the reauthorization of 1992. The common FAF eventually came to be known as the Free Application for Federal Student Aid (FAFSA).

The HEA Reauthorization of 1992 also set in motion the rebuilding of the federal and state data processing systems. The simplification of the FAF and the requirement to use the Congressional Methodology required faster and more efficient ways of processing these applications. The FAF was still a paper form that had to be mailed to the federal processing system. From the time the form was completed to the time the student and the school received the calculated needs analysis could take four to six weeks, sometimes longer.

The results were received by the school in paper format. Schools that had the resources were able to design their own computer programs that could accept data from the federal processing system. A myriad of private companies also designed computer programs that schools could purchase in order to receive the data from the federal processing system. The 1990s saw an explosion of companies and resources that became available to colleges and universities for a cost. What used to take four, six, or eight weeks to process now took an average of two weeks.

It was not only the Financial Aid office that had to adapt to the new technologies that were needed in order to comply with the ever-changing federal and state regulations that involved higher education. The Admissions office, Registrar, Institutional Research, and a variety of other offices now needed to work in true conjunction with each other. Institutions that had developed their own legacy programming now experienced the need for constant reprogramming and hardware updates in order to comply with the regulatory changes.

Enter Y2K: the Year 2000. When the alarm was sounded that companies and institutions needed to reprogram their computer systems before January 1, 2000, a general controlled panic set in. Many computer programs were written to allow only two digits instead of four to denote the year. The fear was what would happen when the year 2000 came and the computer system would reverse the year to the two digits 00. There was then a worldwide effort by companies and institutions to write computer code that could handle Y2K.

Higher education institutions were especially challenged. There would be a need for resources that could handle the computer reprogramming. Some of these institutions were also dealing with aging hardware, a shortage of programmers versed enough in the legacy computer languages, and a variety of computer systems used by various offices in the institutions. One of the answers to the Y2K issues came in the form of companies that recognized the challenges and opportunities and developed what was called integrated processing solutions for higher education.

Most of these companies now offered software in the form of modules that could be purchased together or separately. These modules were programmed to work as integrated parts using what is called a relational database. This type of database stores data points that are related to each other. A Financial Aid module could now have access to Admissions module data and vice versa. The modules that most of these companies offered were the Admissions, Financial Aid, Registrar, Student Accounts, and Business Office. They could each be programmed to access common data points as needed to improve efficiency and accuracy.

Institutions now shifted to a more integrated approach in data processing and the so called "working in a silo mentality" had to be left behind. Higher education now had systems and data analysis tools that transformed what had been a very basic model of the concept of enrollment management. Early admissions deadlines and financial aid awards were now not the only part of the equation for institutional success. The robust data analysis tools that now emerged allowed for very sophisticated parsing of data. Institutions could define what type of student profile they wanted to pursue, how to best leverage institutional, federal, and state financial aid, and even to develop recruitment and retention strategies.

The twenty years since Y2K transformed many aspects of higher education. The financial aid profession was transformed from offices that help students and families apply for and receive financial aid to offices that have to monitor student compliance with diverse requirements from a variety of federal agencies: Selective Service, Homeland Security, Veterans Affairs, Social Security, Internal Revenue Service, Delinquent Loans and Child Support, Federal Felony offenders, among others.

There was now required monitoring of satisfactory academic progress for financial aid recipients and determining refunds and repayment of financial aid funds. While the U.S. Department of Education has tried to simplify the financial aid application, awarding, and disbursement processes, these processes remain complex and financial aid staff spend a good deal of time helping students and families navigate the processes and requirements.

Last but not least, the Financial Aid office is required to verify the information on the FAF if the student is selected by the federal government or the institution for this process of verification. The verification process requires collecting and analyzing federal income tax forms, and other income and asset verification documentation. The Financial Aid office is required to correct any discrepancies before awarding or disbursing federal and state aid.

Many institutions organize the Financial Aid office under their Enrollment Management Division. At these institutions, financial aid student data assists the institution in its student enrollment goals and objectives. The changing landscape of higher education has magnified the role and expectations of the Financial Aid office. The modern Financial Aid office has a diverse group of generalists and specialists. Much of the work of the specialists is in the areas of systems processing, data queries, and technical expertise in the financial aid system.

Funding for the office can become an issue. With dwindling enrollments and reductions in state and federal funding for higher education, many offices are strapped for resources. These offices are expected to maintain a high level of service in the midst of funding and staff reductions. Some aspect of service almost always suffers. Families and students expect good customer service in institutions of higher education.

Higher education is in this sense like any other business. Financial Aid offices are expected to process, award, and disburse aid in set intervals. Financial aid award packages are expected by students and families in a timely manner. The award package can determine the student and families' decision to enroll in the institution. Adequate staffing resources in the Financial Aid office can go a long way in providing the timeliness and level of services that students and families expect.

Most institutions conduct student satisfaction surveys. These surveys may ask the importance that the Financial Aid office played in their decision to attend the institution. These surveys can assist the institution in gauging several aspects of student perceptions of the function and services of the different institutional offices, including Financial Aid. At the end of the day it can be these perceptions that assist an institution in striving for improvement in quality and services.

Throughout the long history of the financial aid profession, its importance and impact on student success cannot be underestimated. From an office of one-on-one financial aid counseling to an office of interacting via social media and processing millions of dollars in federal, state, and institutional funds, this office remains at the core of enrollment management. Technological progress changed the profession as well as expectations. The Financial Aid office should always have a seat at the enrollment management table.

In retrospect, having a seat at the enrollment management table elevated and challenged Financial Aid offices. The Financial Aid office became part of a team. The relationship between the offices of Admissions, Registrar, and Financial Aid transformed a once basic collegial relationship to one of true collaboration and sharing common institutional goals and objectives that were now a part of the institution's recruitment and retention objectives. The team effort encouraged an analysis of how each office was operating and what processes and practices could improve.

This analysis led to a prioritization of improvements based on available resources. An example of this is the "lean process improvement" that the Financial Aid office at the University of Wisconsin Oshkosh undertook. The goal was to increase efficiency and turnaround time in processing and awarding financial aid. If the office could reduce the time between the receipt of financial aid information and awarding and sending the award letter to students, the expectation was that there would be an increase in award acceptance by students which could also increase the volume of acceptance of admission offers.

The lean process improvement analysis showed that the turnaround time could be reduced from five to three days if some workflow adjustments were made. This process change would also involve the Student Accounts office at the point when disbursement of student aid could be made. This team approach was a success. Financial aid award offers' turnaround time was reduced and admission acceptance offers saw an uptick. From then on, each of these offices was constantly challenged to self-analysis and improvement.

At the end of the day, when and how improvements could and would be made had a direct correlation with what resources were available. The most valuable resources at institutions of higher education are its human resources and its funding levels. The mantra became to do more with less in times of decreasing revenue streams and hiring freezes. From the seat of the Financial Aid office at the University of Wisconsin Oshkosh, the loss of several positions and a decreased operating budget affected the amount of quality time that could be spent on one-on-one financial aid counseling and customer service to students, parents, and the community at large.

This experience is most likely shared by many other Financial Aid offices. Financial Aid directors will always dream and hope for that additional financial aid counselor or systems specialist who could enhance the level of service to students and assist with process improvements. They are and must be the best advocates for the financial aid profession and the institutions that they serve.

ESSAY: DAVID MCMILLIAN—
BOOTS ON THE GROUND

There are few offices that can impact a college or university's bottom line more than Financial Aid. The institutional risk associated with the Financial Aid office is unique and vast. Federal program reviews, scholarship management, and discounting are just a few of the challenges that financial aid offices must face. This office can also provide data critical to enrollment projection, budget expenditures, and gross revenue. Data points such as FAFSA filing rates, Expected Family Contribution trends, and financial needs gaps are essential indicators for evaluating student enrollment behavior. This essay examines strategies to mitigate risk within the Financial Aid office and how to use financial aid data to inform the college's decisions.

Every college should evaluate the risk to the institution. One of the most considerable risks to a college that receives federal student aid is the threat of the U.S. Department of Education fining or suspending the college from federal student aid. It is the whole college's responsibility to maintain compliance; however, that responsibility, more often than not, falls on the director of Financial Aid. While the Financial Aid office usually is the first office to know about changes in federal regulation, these changes may directly impact other departments. Examples of federal regulations outside of Financial Aid are: missing student notification, enrollment reporting, and Cleary Act reporting.

Another risk that arises out of the Financial Aid office is overdiscounting. Unfunded discounting (unfunded scholarships) is a useful and necessary process to provide a pathway to enrollment for students. Unchecked discounting can lead to budget shortfalls, even with record enrollment. It is crucial that enrollment management leaders and budget leaders work together to have a plan that maximizes enrollment with an understanding of the actual cost of the discounting. All parties should regularly review expenditures and enrollment to ensure that budget projections align with real-time data. Nothing can sour a college president's mood quicker than hearing that they have a record class but did not hit the net tuition revenue.

Data provides college leaders with the tools necessary to make informed decisions. One of the main data creators within a college is the Office of Financial Aid. What is useful about the data produced is that it provides decision-making with information from both outside and inside the institution. Internal information includes financial aid applications, interactions with the Financial Aid office, and financial aid eligibility. External information includes family finance information and student financial need.

For colleges that rely on federal aid, the FAFSA filing rate is critical for identifying issues early. When enrollment managers see FAFSA rates below yearly averages, this should be a warning that difficult times lie ahead. The reduction in the filing rate means that the college is not getting its best offer out to its prospective students. By not getting the best offer to prospective students the college may experience a reduction in new student matriculation. Other issues from a dip in the FAFSA filing rate could include an incoming class that is planning on attending but do not have a plan for paying tuition and fees.

According to nerdwallet.com, 37 percent of the graduating high school class of 2018 did not complete their FAFSA, leaving an estimated 2.6 billion dollars in gift aid on the table.[18] Ensuring the college presents the best financial aid package available increases students' likelihood of depositing and matriculating. The challenge is getting students to apply and complete the process. According to the National Center for Education Statistics, reasons students did not complete a FAFSA are: not expecting to qualify for federal aid; did not want to take on student debt; did not know they could complete the FAFSA, or thought it would be too much work.[19]

Increasing FAFSA filing rates should be the goal of the whole campus not just the Financial Aid office. Enrollment managers must engage student-facing offices such as Admissions, Athletics, Advising, and other student-support offices to motivate prospective and returning students to start the FAFSA process early. One strategy is to have the director of Financial Aid meet with the recruiting staff in Admissions and Athletics to review changes in federal, state, and institutional aid programs. These meetings ensure that recruiters have a general understanding of the financial aid process and provide additional avenues for students to understand the importance of completing the FAFSA.

Another strategy is to share FAFSA filing rates with select partners to ensure that the campus works in tandem on a FAFSA filing message. It is important to create benchmarks to evaluate the effectiveness of FAFSA filing campaigns. Enrollment managers should then extrapolate this information to help develop class projections. Using historical data to identify matriculation rates and returning student rates provides enrollment managers with useful information during budget times. At the end of the academic year, enrollment managers and campus partners should meet weekly to review filing rates across different student populations in order to target outreach to particular students.

Financial aid data can also help with retention modeling. Return FAFSA filers, loss of scholarships, and satisfactory academic progress (SAP) issues are all data points that help enrollment managers' projections. It is important to recognize that financial aid data does not happen in a vacuum, and it is crucial to bring student services offices together to collaborate.

For example, Financial Aid data helps with retention by identifying students who have a FAFSA for the current year but have yet to complete a FAFSA for the upcoming year. This information, combined with transcript requests, can identify students who will most likely not be returning to the College. Another tactic to increase retention is to create a process that requires students who fail to meet SAP to work with academic counselors or tutoring services to provide academic support for academically at-risk students.

The Piedmont College Vice President of Enrollment Management convened a group of staff and faculty that included the Registrar, Admissions, Financial Aid, Student Accounts, and Athletics. This "Vortex" group met regularly to discuss retention of students. This committee provided data gathered in each office unit, and used that information to evaluate retention efforts on an individual student level. The Vortex was able to identify students who were teetering on failure and provide the student with resources to help with success.

The information gathered and analyzed from this committee allowed the College to identify data markers that helped model retention rates. Some of those indicators are transcript requests, not meeting with the adviser, not completing a FAFSA for the upcoming academic year, and being disconnected from their athletic team. This committee was an action-oriented committee that was responsive to student needs and offered a positive first step.

The information the Vortex creates can then be used by division leaders. By breaking down trends and using a longitudinal data approach these leaders can let data inform their policy construction. This approach helps identify ongoing changes within the student body. These changes can include the student population's ability to pay (financial need), changes in the percentage of students receiving the Federal Pell Grant, and changes in the number of students who meet SAP, among others.

Once changes are identified, the administration can implement policies and initiatives to help mitigate negative trends or encourage positive movement. A real-life example of this is creating a 3 + 2 program that leads to a degree at partner colleges. Piedmont College noticed that students majoring in the applied physics program transferred to a larger public university to complete a degree. The Dean of Arts and Sciences saw this and worked with that institution to create matriculation agreements that would allow the student to receive a degree at both institutions once the course work had been completed.

Data can influence policy on a macro-level by evaluating student need and percentage of Pell Grant students at the college. To calculate federal need, a student must complete a FAFSA. The calculation uses the college's Cost of Attendance less the Estimated Financial Contribution, calculated by the FAFSA. Each college needs to know its median need and percentage of the student body that qualifies for the federal Pell Grant populations. These variables give enrollment managers an insight into how the student body will react to tuition and fee increases.

Colleges with a large student need but low Pell populations are sensitive to tuition increases. This may seem counterintuitive; however, in this situation, you are looking at students with low EFCs that do not receive additional funding from the Pell Grant. Therefore, any tuition increase falls directly on the student or their family, who may not have the resources. With Pell-eligible students, tuition increases may be offset by Pell Grant increases, should Congress appropriate additional funds. Tuition increases are necessary to provide colleges with sufficient resources; however, governing boards should be diligent in reviewing the increase rate, knowing that it will impact retention. This is especially true at colleges with a high need population.

All colleges create data. That information should inform assumptions, drive predictions, and set goals. It is up to each institution to determine if they will use that data to inform their decision-making. Goals established with data are attainable, and predictions made using informed decision making are more reliable. These goals and projections have benchmarks and can be measured. FAFSA filing rates can be measured year over year. Changes in variables when the model fails can be identified. It is imperative that those individuals who are closest to the data work in collaboration to create a framework to assess the information, and then use that information to inform decision-making. This approach will ensure that decisions have accountability and are in the best interest of the college.

NOTES

1. Alexis Pope and Susan Davies. "Influencing Institutional Expectations through Organizational Leadership and Contextual Data." *Strategic Enrollment Management Quarterly 8*(2): Summer 2020, 3.
2. Karen Doss Bowman. "Shifting Demographics." *Trusteeship:* Association of Governing Boards of Universities and Colleges. (March/April, 2020) *28*(2): 24.
3. Ibid. Pope and Davies, 5–7.
4. Erik Brynjolfsson and Kristina Steffenson McElheran. "Data-Driven Decision Making in Action." *MIT IDE Research Brief 2017*(1). Retrieved October 9, 2020, from http://ide.mit.edu/publications/data-driven-decision-making-action.
5. David Stuart and Todd Nordstrom. "Are You Asking the Right Question?" *Forbes,* Forbes Magazine. Retrieved October 9, 2020, from http://www.forbes.com/sites/davidstuart/archive.
6. Peter M. Lee. "Lies, Damned Lies and Statistics." University of York. Retrieved October 9, 2020, from https://www.york.ac.uk/depts/maths/histstat/lies.htm.
7. Michael Berman. "New Life for Legacy Systems." *Educause Review.* Retrieved October 9, 2020, from https://er.educause.edu/articles/2019/8/new-life-for-legacy-systems.
8. https://nces.ed.gov/ipeds/about-ipeds.
9. https://nces.ed.gov/.
10. https://nces.ed.gov/collegenavigator.
11. Adam McCann. "Best Colleges Ranking." *WalletHub* (October 21, 2019). Retrieved October 9, 2020, from https://wallethub.com/edu/e/best-colleges-in-the-us-ranking/40748/.
12. https://www.usnews.com/best-colleges.
13. https://www.princetonreview.com/college-rankings?rankings=party-schools.
14. https://www.economicmodeling.com/.
15. https://www.hanoverresearch.com/.
16. https://www.ruffalonl.com/.
17. https://www.airweb.org/.

18. *McGurran, Brianna. "Students Missed Out on $2.6 Billion in Free College Money." *NerdWallet*, November 13, 2019, www.nerdwallet.com/blog/2018-fafsa-study/.

19. Bahr, Steven et al. "Stats in Brief: Why Didn't Students Complete a Free Application for Federal Student Aid (FAFSA)? A Detailed Look." U.S. Department of Education: National Center for Education Statistics, December 2018, https://nces.ed.gov/pubs2018/2018061.pdf.

Chapter 2

Admissions, Recruiting, and Marketing

The people we hire in our Admissions and Marketing offices have incredibly difficult jobs. Not only is this new and more diverse generation different in their expectations, needs, and concerns than the previous generation, their parents are playing an ever increasing and demanding role. Beyond responding to the Gen Z student population, those folks in Admissions and Marketing must also tailor their approaches to an expanding nontraditional student population with entirely different needs and expectations. Finally, add employer needs, alumni wishes, and emerging technology and social media to this volatile mix, and you have institutional staff scrapping for resources and for their sanity.

A quick reminder of the characteristics of our new Gen Z population is appropriate. This increasingly diverse student body has significant financial worries, expect their college degrees to help them attain stable jobs, and want their degrees to be relevant. While this new generation is technologically connected, they feel more isolated than ever before and have growing mental health concerns. Their parents have been their sources of support and their decision-makers. When they enter our college campuses, they need support: ranging from career services to counseling services, and from tutoring to advising.

Gen Z are self-starters and want to be entrepreneurial; they like to find the answers themselves at any time, day or night. Gen Z student Josh Miller explained, "successfully engaging with Generation Z requires striking a balance between conversing directly and engaging online. Both are important, and we need to feel connected in both ways to be fully satisfied."[1] Since these new students are career-focused, they are looking for universities with clearly identified (with success metrics) learning outcomes[2] expressing job placements and graduate school placements. To help them prepare, they are looking for robust internship opportunities.[3] They are also looking for financial transparency and value for their money.

A quick note should be added here about the group after Gen Z. Believe it or not, they already have a designation—Gen Alpha. Genevieve Shaw Brown explains that this group born after 2010 will be even more connected digitally, more geographically mobile, and thus more extensively connected to one another across the globe."[4]

Every office of Admissions and every office of Marketing have been tested to their limits with the COVID-19 pandemic. The campus visit has been the sine qua non for every admissions recruiter from the beginning of time. This primary yield strategy came to a screeching halt during spring break 2020. The instant switch to multiple technology and communication platforms was required overnight. Quite frankly, such strategic shifts have been unparalleled in recent memory.

Many strategies have been so successful, however, that they will continue in the years to come. For example, virtual campus visits will henceforth be an opportunity for all prospective students. More videoconferencing will be used, as well as other virtual yet personalized communication strategies. Live presentations can be archived for students to review at a time of their choosing.[5]

The coronavirus pandemic altered admissions standards and protocols in myriad ways. For example, the SAT and ACT normed testing services were largely inaccessible from spring through fall 2020. This forced universities to abandon standardized testing requirements and move even more toward holistic approaches. Vice president emeritus Robert Massa of Dickinson College further noted that admissions officers will now do more videoconferencing with prospective students and their high school counselors. Massa went on to explain that in order to meet employer needs, admissions staff will need to look for students who are good at problem-solving, teamwork, critical thinking, creativity, and exhibit intellectual curiosity. Such expectations will put more of an onus on the personal interview and written essays.[6]

As has been noted elsewhere, parents of Gen Z play a critical role in the final choice of which school to attend. This requires new approaches to communicating and engaging with parents. It was stated earlier that this group of students is more diverse than ever and the discrepancy in families' ability to pay for college is greater than ever before, as well. In fact, Hispanic and African-American families have family incomes roughly only 60 percent of their white counterparts. Affluent parents think of their sons and daughters as children who still need help, while less affluent parents feel their sons and daughters are grown up and can take care of themselves.

Both affluent, and less affluent and first-generation families have different expectations and needs according to Hamilton, Roksa, and Nielsen. These authors indicate that affluent parents seek institutions with competitive academic programs and special social programming. They also focus on career planning and connections for internships. On the other hand, less affluent and first-generation parents don't feel equipped to help their progeny to navigate academic and support programs. Nor do they have established connections to extended social systems and professional employment opportunities.[7]

Two final points need to be made before we move into the following practitioner-expert essays. First, the most significant, growing, and stable student demographic of today and tomorrow is the nontraditional student—the student over twenty-five years of age who likely is concurrently busy in the workplace. Projections indicate this growing population will pursue more higher education opportunities in the years to come.[8]

Admissions and marketing staff need to develop relationships with this population by engaging them where they are—at work. Direct connections with Human Resources offices will be essential. But equally important, if not more so, is making connections with employers through advisory boards and by developing curricular offerings to meet the emerging needs of the workplace, and subsequently building student internships and credit for prior learning.

Second, graduate student admissions will begin to see corresponding demographic shifts and student expectations as noted above, in a few short years. They need to begin to make the necessary adjustments now, in order to be ready when this new generational wave hits them. While the graduate student enrollment grew significantly between 2000 and 2017 (from 2,000,000 to 3,000,000 students nationwide) the expected traditional population increase will only add 100,000 more students across the nation by 2028.[9]

The following essays are written by Cindy Peterson and Kathleen Carter. Between the two of them, they have several decades of experience leading undergraduate and graduate admissions staff—they have seen it all. They will explain the work of their offices, policies and protocols, and the ebbs and flows of the admission cycle—different for each group. Even more importantly, they will describe initiatives they have led, as well as their wish lists to take their work to the next level.

ESSAY: CINDY PETERSON—THE UNDERGRADUATE ADMISSIONS LIFE CYCLE

Finding, attracting, and enrolling the right students is more challenging than ever, making each stage of the enrollment journey critical for the prospective undergraduate student and their family. With a shift in the demographics of graduating high school students over the next five to ten years, admissions offices must optimize their recruitment strategies. From targeting applications to maximizing matriculation rates to staving off summer melt, enrollment funnel management is key to an office of admissions' success.

The Admissions Funnel

The most common model is that of an upright funnel (see Figure 2.1) where names of prospects and inquiries and stealth applications (those who apply with no communication) pour into the top with the goal of moving the most qualified and engaged students through the funnel to enrollment. Prospects are typically generated by buying names from college board and ACT/NRCCUA using academic criteria (high school GPA and test scores), and majors.

A special marketing plan and communication flow takes place at this level, seeking those who inquire about the college, moving them down the funnel to the "Inquiry" phase. Once at the Inquiry phase, a more robust and personalized communication flow begins, encouraging calls to action such as a visit to campus and application. At the Applicant phase communications pivot to completion of applications, calling for transcripts, test scores, and essays. The next phase of the funnel is Admitted status; strategic messaging at this phase is critical and includes correspondence from people such as the president, alumni board members, academic deans, academic department chairs, current students, and parents of current students.

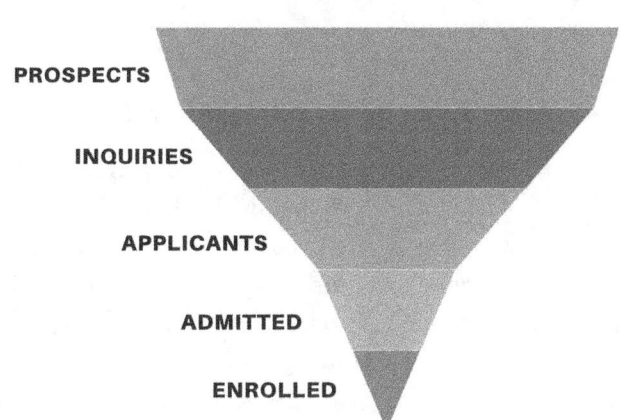

Figure 2.1 Enrollment Funnel. Nikki Blanchard

Gaining commitment once a student is admitted requires multiple engagements via text, email, print, phone calling, video chats, in-person interviews, and so much more. Once commitment is garnered and deposits are received, student engagement becomes critical to prevent what admissions offices refer to as melt—losing enrollments after student deposits. Using social media platforms such as YouTube, Instagram, Snapchat, and Facebook (for parents) is vital at this phase. Connecting students and parents to the college community and building those relationships helps solidify their commitment to enroll.

CRM (Constituent Relationship Management) System

Our college recognized our technology solutions were limited without a CRM. Understanding the need for personalized, creative, and segmented messaging throughout each phase of a student's journey through the enrollment funnel, we needed a robust system to help us manage the complex messaging automation. We needed event management solutions, campus visit software, text messaging capability, and more. The decision to implement a CRM tool that was compatible with the existing SIS was strategic, and within the first year yielded a significant increase in the conversion of inquiries to applications, and completed applications to admitted students. Selecting the TargetX Recruitment Suite has allowed us to empower admissions productivity with intuitive, mobile-first CRM functionality designed for higher education.

SEARCH—A Critical Piece to Recruitment Strategy

In 2018, heading into the recruitment cycle, we recognized our inquiry pool for Fall 2019 was 6,000 students, well below the national average of 10,000 to 12,000 names. It was clear that the student search names we bought the year before had not converted to inquiries at the rate needed to achieve future enrollment goals. Student Search is one of the most effective ways to reach prospective traditional students. However, few schools have the resources to conduct their own search effectively. Sophisticated search includes mail, publications, digital marketing and advertising, telephone contacts, and email campaigns. These programs include 10 to 15 contacts with prospective students and parents, include a value-added first response offering, and are conducted year-round.

To improve our search response, we selected a vendor who had proved tremendous success with other private liberal arts colleges. After a comprehensive review of five years of applicant-to-enrollment data, a marketing firm provided us with a detailed analysis of the potential markets in which we should invest resources to recruit. Despite COVID's impact, our inquiry pool increased to over 9,000 names in our first few months of using a specialized search partner, generating a stronger, more qualified pool of applicants.

Communications Flow

If you are not a household-name institution, you are at a disadvantage in that you must educate students about your college. The institution's story must be communicated well and often. Institutions need a robust and comprehensive communication program designed to inform and convince students, parents, teachers, and high school counselors that you are an outstanding institution and an excellent fit for the right student. With that in mind we worked to develop an effective communication plan.

The goal of our communication plan was to achieve targeted conversion rates at each stage of the admissions funnel from the point of inquiry through enrollment. The communication flow builds the student's interest in the college from low at the point of inquiry to high at the time of final decision. To work successfully, our communication flow combines and integrates written, electronic, and personal communication over the period when prospective students are making their college choice. The process involves a long (18 to 24 months) relationship between the institution and the prospective student. The primary job of a professional admissions administrator, advisor, or recruiter is to manage the relationships with inquiries and applicants.

Research shows that, when students inquire to a college or university, they respond best to emotional messages that communicate feelings rather than simply facts. Students base their decisions to apply for admission on cognitive information (e.g., program availability, sense of quality, distance from home, and cost) that allows them to compare one college/university to another. The final decision to enroll requires a combination of both emotional and cognitive information but weighs more favorably on the emotional. Cognitive messages inform and educate, while the emotional messages illicit interest and build commitment. This twofold model must be used when designing key recruitment messages and themes.

The type and timing of the message are essential to raising the level of student interest, supplying information they look for, relieving anxiety, and building commitment and engagement. Emotional messages drive student interest, therefore inquiry-generating methods should not try to overcommunicate information. Feelings of excitement, a buzz around campus life, and student engagement must be conveyed and will result in a request for more information about the college/university.

Recruitment Strategy

Key strategies and tactics for recruitment and marketing efforts of prospective first-year students include, but are not limited to, publications (student marketing search pieces, Viewbook, etc.), email communications, website management, text messaging, calling mobile phones rather than land lines, embedding videos on the website, and within email communications/newsletters. As part of our yield strategy, admissions advisors received a day-long training session from the office of Financial Aid, titled "Conducting Financial Award Letter Follow-Up Conversations with Students and Their Families."

Given the high percentage of first-generation students and Pell recipients who attend our college, it is especially important that we supply more information and support around the financial aid process. First-generation students list cost and financial aid as more important reasons in their enrollment decision than non-first-generation students.

Added recruitment/marketing efforts include the use of social media, digital advertising, online chat, virtual tours, aid/scholarship calculator on the college website, and in-person meetings on and off campus. Parent communications are vital in the communications flow, supplying outreach to some of the most crucial influencers of higher education. We have found that adding a parent page to the website and creating a parent Facebook group have also been essential yield strategies.

Campus Visit Program

A campus visit program is one of the key components of a strategic recruitment plan. Personalized on-campus visits provide prospective students and their families the opportunity to meet with an admissions advisor, a faculty member based on their academic interest, a financial aid advisor, and a personal tour guide. Those who do visit campus have a very real interest in attending the institution, which is why the campus tour should fan those flames of interest, conveying the new and exciting "student experience."

From the moment the student arrives in the admissions lobby seeing their name on the big screen to the final closing session, a campus tour is often the "make or break" decision for prospective students and their families. Sending the student home with a thank you gift (t-shirt) and an information package holding a Majors brochure and Viewbook creates a positive and memorable ending to their visit and adds talking points for their ride home.

Campus Events

Campus events produce strong yield, especially when they provide outreach to specific populations. One example is our Dia de la Familia, an open house dedicated to the Hispanic community. Another is a Fine Arts College Experience (FACE), which provides high school juniors and seniors interested in music, theater, or the visual arts the opportunity to attend classes, stay in the residence hall with an assigned host, and audition for fine arts scholarships.

Key to the success of any campus tour or campus event, however, is strong faculty involvement. The feedback most families give at the end of a tour or event centers around having had the benefit of meeting with a professor or a school dean. With that said, we are very intentional in selecting and training faculty and deans for effective prospective student visits. The faculty meeting is often the most impactful part of a student's visit to our campus.

Preventing Summer Melt—Creating an Admissions Vortex

For those who work in college admissions it would not be summer without the melt. Suddenly that expected class has dwindled by 15 percent or more and you ask yourself, what do we have in our bag of tricks that could offer solutions to prevent that melt?

First things first. Discover the patterns that appear around the stories of melted students. Lower than expected financial aid is often the glaring flag that gets raised first. The excitement of receiving the celebratory acceptance letter wears off quickly if the financial aid falls short of what they expected or needed. Perhaps our school was their backup plan and they pick their first choice. These are stories heard repeatedly. First-generation students are most at risk in the summer. They meet more hurdles than their peers from degree-earned households and require more direct communication from various offices on campus throughout the summer.

On many college campuses a silo approach to enrollment management is the model. However, when it comes to preventing summer melt those silos must come down and be replaced with bridges, giving access to information and communications from each office in a coordinated effort. One solution we implemented was an Admissions Vortex—an ad-hoc committee made up of representatives from every office that has a stake in a student's ultimate enrollment.

Faculty, staff, and administrators campus-wide meet weekly to review communications, including the timing and tone of messages, the audience to which they are sent (parents and/or students), and the calls to action they solicit. From the Admissions office asking for final high school transcripts, to the orientation coordinator urging students to complete an online orientation course, to the Business office seeking signatures on the student's financial statement, keeping deposited students and their parents connected to a map of "next steps" are critical to helping stave off summer melt. With the efforts set in place after a Fall 2019 First Year melt at our college of 11 percent, the Fall 2020 melt dropped to 9 percent, just below the national average for private four-year institutions.

One example of parent and student engagement messaging follows below. The roadmap (see Figure 2.2) offers a family a visual representation of the steps needed to enroll in classes. It walks students through the various requirements from offices across the campus. It offers a comprehensive list of "next steps" for new students.

Our Roadmap to Becoming a Part of the Pride

The absolute thrill of any Admissions office is "move-in" day when new students arrive on campus and the baton is passed to the Office of Student Success and Engagement. Once that "hand-off" occurs, the Admissions team evaluates and assesses their annual strategy and sets their sites on the next recruitment cycle. The journey begins anew.

ESSAY: KATHLEEN CARTER—THE WORLD OF GRADUATE ADMISSIONS

The first steps in the Graduate Admissions cycle are recruiting and marketing; therefore, the work in the Office of Graduate Admissions is a cyclical endeavor. Before the internet became the first place most students go for information, we could reach prospective students by placing our recruitment advertising in local newspapers and on local radio stations. But whatever the medium, we must capture the attention of prospective students and show them who we are and how we are different from other competing institutions. And we must do this using a variety of platforms.

The Office of Graduate Admissions must present a pertinent, quality proposal showing value for the cost to prospective graduate students. To do this we must use both traditional and online/social media marketing. As 90 percent of Piedmont University's graduate enrollments are teacher-educators, we explain how our education programs are tailored to be specific to school district needs; and, we show how our MBA program enhances the student's knowledge to be able meet their needs in more rural as well as urban areas. Student testimonials showcase what our programs offer and are important for applicants to see someone like them become successful.

To help us identify factors that make our graduate programs stand out from those of other institutions, we surveyed the students currently enrolled in our programs. We asked what they liked or disliked in our programs, and for suggestions to enhance what is currently offered. Getting the answers to these few simple questions helped us shape how we in Graduate Admissions approach our marketing and recruiting plans. Also, we found talking with prospective students at graduate fairs to be one of the most informative ways to find what programs are desired.

Checklist to being a Piedmont Lion!

Use this checklist as a resource to ensure you complete all the steps to be a Piedmont Lion!

BEFORE SUMMER ORIENTATION

- [x] Be Admitted to Piedmont College
- [ ] Pay your Deposit (Use QR code for link)
- [ ] Register for summer orientation- https://www.piedmont.edu/orientation
- [ ] Set up their student LIONS email- *only after deposit is paid, and may take up to one week to be processed.*
- [ ] Complete the Financial Agreement and FAFSA

If living on campus, complete housing forms:

- [ ] Student Information Form (to be submitted online)
- [ ] Housing Questionnaire (to be submitted online)
- [ ] Health Services Immunization Record (to be printed and completed by your health care provider, includes MCV4 shot and TB test)
- [ ] Complete the "Please Don't Snore" profile sent to the LIONS account

- [ ] Send FINAL high school transcripts, AP Scores, CLEP scores and official Dual Enrollment transcripts to Undergraduate Admissions
- [ ] Download the Piedmont College App from the App Store or Google Play Store
- [ ] Enroll or waive out of the SHIP insurance (You will recieve information to LIONS email July 2020)

BEFORE MOVE IN DAY

- [ ] Complete Everfi survey
- [ ] Once registered for classes, purchase/order required books

IMPORTANT PHONE NUMBERS

ADMISSIONS: 706-776-0103

ATHLETICS: 706-778-8500, X-1358

STUDENT ACCOUNTS: 706-776-0101

FINANCIAL AID: 706-776-0114

REGISTRAR: 706-778-8500, X-1112

RESIDENTIAL LIVING:
706-778-8500, X-1357

STUDENT AFFAIRS
(SHIP & Housing Forms):
706-894-4209

SUMMER ORIENTATION COORDINATOR:
706-778-8500, X-2834

IMPORTANT DATES

Monday, August 3
Move in for SAIL participants

Thursday, August 6, 2020
Move in for all other first-year students

August 6 - 16
Welcome Week

Monday, August 10
Classes Begin

Use this QR code to go to our website for links to all the forms!

Figure 2.2 The Admissions Roadmap Checklist.

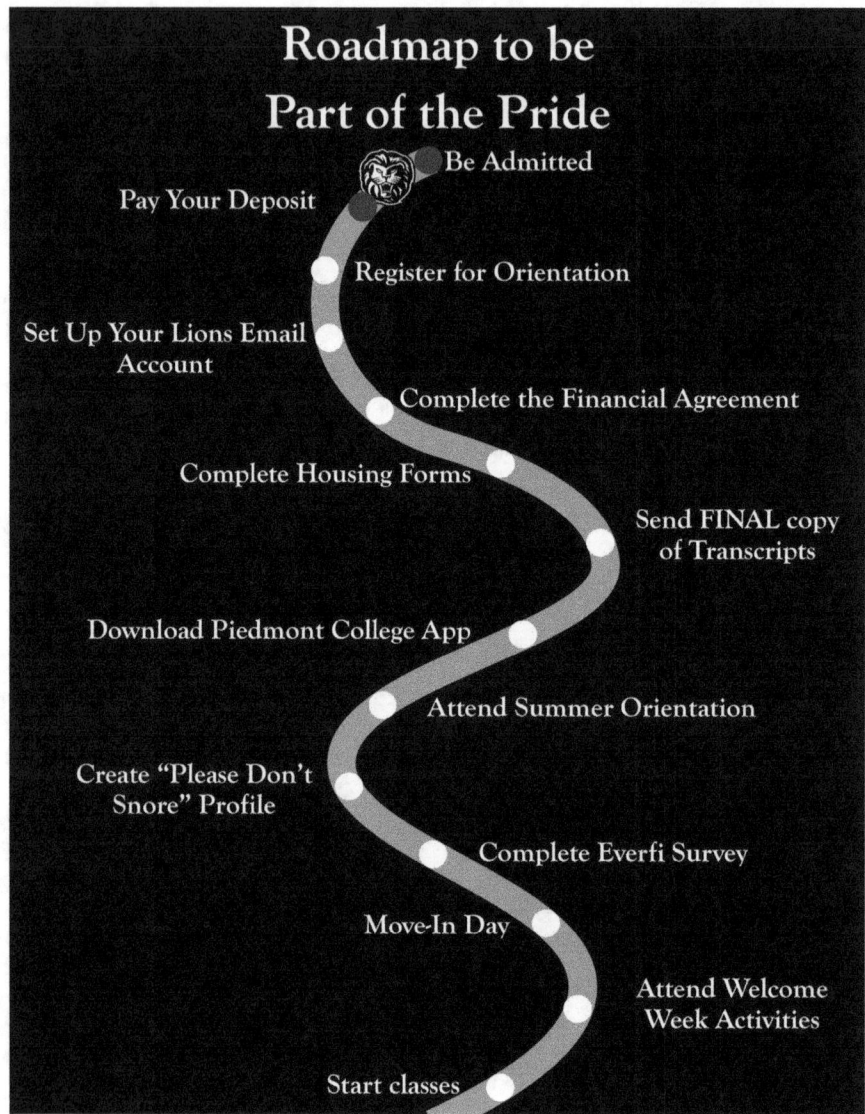

Figure 2.2 *(Continued)*.

Using information from the surveys sent to prospective and current students and conversations at graduate fairs, we learned which programs, such as the two-track Counseling degree and Business/Education certificates, have the greatest interest. From that input, we then can inform our deans which programs should be promoted with senior administration. By gaining these insights into what prospects are seeking, our office is able to stay up to date with current program demands.

Our Admissions staff is aware that prospective graduate students are interested in specific degree programs, not necessarily the institution offering the programs. In other words, our students are less worried about where they get their degree and are more concerned about the program of study. Many of the graduate student prospects are working full time. Because of this, the Graduate Admission's recruitment process must be different from that of Undergraduate Admissions. We recruit students from the area for our programs, as we are a regionally recognized university.

Our small recruiting and advertising budget is allocated to give us the best return for the money—what we believe is the biggest "bang for our buck." To streamline the process in our small Graduate Admissions office, one staff member is dedicated to recruitment duties for on-campus students, in addition to other responsibilities. One of the best and most far-reaching advertising modes we use is radio spots.

These informative spots are broadcast multiple times during the heaviest driving times (7:30–8:00 a.m. and 5:00–6:00 p.m.). By repeating these spots many times, listeners become familiar with the institution's name and its offerings. They begin to relate to the speaker and the message even when they are not paying particular attention.

We learned from many years of recruiting that our display of brochures and rack cards really sets our institution apart from others. These glossy publications with colorful pictures of graduate students participating in our programs catch the eye and encourage people to pick them up. Once the prospect's attention is captured by the pictures, they can read the information provided about our campus and our programs. At recruitment fairs and events attended by hundreds of prospective students, booths with the glossiest and most colorful brochures on display have the most interest from the attendees.

Students in today's world are digitally minded: therefore, we must meet prospective students where they are—online. Social media campaigns are a must in today's higher education marketing. Our office promotes graduate offerings on Facebook, Instagram, and through Twitter and Snapchat. Our online messages are updated at least weekly, if not daily. In our office the same person who is responsible for recruitment duties also is responsible for keeping these social media messages updated. Changing messages often keep prospects interested and coming back to the page again and again.

Working with the Office of Advancement and Marketing to develop advertising for specific graduate programs makes it easier to attract students interested in those areas. We know the information presented must be relevant to the searcher, so what we present to a prospective MBA student is different from that we use to target an Education student.

For the Education student we would concentrate on showing how getting an advanced degree will benefit them. Upgrading their teaching credentials may provide a pay increase and expanded employment opportunities. The MBA student would be shown how their advanced degree would help with networking opportunities, job promotion, and a higher salary. We are continually looking to determine the needs of our marketplace.

Our university's website has been revamped several times over the past twenty years. Each update has moved us closer to what our faculty and staff feel best promotes their message. When the website started, we were a small regional college and a couple of information pages sufficed. Now we are a much larger regional university and need separate webpages for each department and degree. Our website must stay current visually for prospective students to feel that our technology is contemporary.

Even knowing most of our prospective graduate students research our programs through the internet, it is often difficult to have any Graduate information on the front page of the institution's website. The focus is on promoting the Undergraduate program. This is understandable as the university's primary focus is the undergrad population. Even so, there does need to be space for presenting Graduate programing. Maintaining a link on the main website page that will allow the user to go directly to the Graduate page works best. The fewer clicks the user must make the better.

Prospective students often call the Admissions office to ask very specific questions when they cannot find the answer online. Knowing this helps with developing our marketing decisions. Our university faculty members are an integral part of developing our recruiting program. Maintaining a good working relationship with different offices on campus is crucial. In addition to the four different colleges, we work closely with the offices of Advancement and Marketing, Financial Aid, the Business, and the Registrar. We all work together to make the applicant/student experience as positive as we can.

Each semester we schedule meetings with participating faculty and ask the following questions: What sets your program apart from similar programs offered at other institutions? How will this degree benefit the student? What are the future prospects for those who graduate from this degree program? Are you willing to actively help recruit with the Graduate Admissions staff to promote your program? This last question is possibly the most important. We find most prospective students want to interact with someone who is part of the program in which they are interested. As busy as our faculty are, they will carve out time to meet with prospective students.

Twenty-three years ago, our university realized there was a need for our state's teacher population to have a way to upgrade their teaching certificates while continuing to teach full-time. These upgrades provide not only advanced education but pay increases, and greater retirement benefits, too. For this population to be served, a program would need to be both convenient and accessible. It was a special niche filled by the development of our very successful Off-Campus Education Program. This was the start of an enormous influx of students at the graduate level. It was so popular, there was a time when our graduate student numbers outpaced our undergraduate population.

Years ago, we found offering our program at the teachers' own school districts allowed a large cohort of teachers the ability to obtain a higher degree without needing to drive to our main campus location. Instead, the thousands of teachers we have served through this program had the opportunity to attend university classes in their own school districts. It was possible for these teachers to walk down their school's hallway to a classroom to attend graduate school. And it gave our university the ability to meet the needs of students who normally would be too far away from our campus to attend graduate school.

Recruiting for these cohorts of teachers brings its own set of very distinct needs. Each individual school district's needs and wants must be provided by our program. Part of the popularity for these cohorts of teachers is our university's desire to work with each district's self-identified School Improvement Projects, their scheduling needs, and building usage permissions.

Our university Admissions staff ascertains the district's specific school improvement topics by working with a district contact, usually the Assistant

Superintendent, and determines how our university might help their teachers prepare to meet these needs. These programs will lead to the granting of either a Master of Education or an Education Specialist degree. Permission is needed from the school district to present our program to the teachers; once permission is granted the work of recruitment begins.

Our Graduate Admissions staff is very small, only five people. Traveling to school locations throughout the state recruiting teachers for the graduate programs is very time consuming. These recruitment presentations are given after regular school hours. The person on our staff dedicated to recruiting presents most of these teacher recruiting programs. Two other staff members will travel to make presentations when needed.

Even with our small staff, each semester we have succeeded in recruiting an average of fifteen new cohort groups. We have an average of fifty groups running concurrently each semester. There are numerous details to keep organized for these programs to run smoothly. If we had one more staff member dedicated to recruiting, we could recruit more cohort groups. For every teacher we recruit, someone in the office must manage the applicant's file. This usually entails multiple phone calls and/or emails with the applicant to help complete the file for acceptance.

There are many software programs that will send out automated emails to applicants throughout the application cycle. We had the opportunity to use such a system. After working with the program for about a month, we recognized the importance of personal interaction. Now all of our email correspondence is specific to the applicant.

A software program can automatically put in a name on an email, but we think the entire email language should show the Graduate Admissions staff is working specifically for this applicant. Customer service is an important aspect of Admissions and we try to always remember who our customer is. We want the applicants and students to feel we are here to work with each of them as individuals.

Offering graduate classes throughout the state in multiple locations means we must depend on part-time instructors. At the inception of the Off-Campus Education Program it was decided to employ a mix of our own university instructors, current schoolteachers, central office personnel, and assistant superintendents and superintendents, who have terminal degrees in the content areas they are to teach. Our instructors bring real life experience to the teachers they are instructing. Teachers appreciate learning from someone who understands the issues they deal with on a daily basis.

The impact of reaching this number of teacher leaders in our state is immense. Since the inception of the cohort delivery model in 1997, we have granted graduate degrees to over 15,000 teachers. Granting graduate degrees to teachers who live and teach in rural areas, who otherwise might not have had the chance to attend graduate school, not only helps the teachers' financial futures but also brings current teaching strategies to their school districts, to which they may not have been exposed otherwise.

It is rewarding to see the large number of Teacher of the Year awards presented to former students of the cohort programs. Graduate enrollment depends on the former students promoting our programs. The best recruiters are the students themselves—who have experienced the rewards from completing the program.

When our off-campus programs began in 1997, recruiting was conducted solely by face-to-face meetings, graduate fairs, and newspaper advertisements. We were able to enroll many students because there were no other options available to this population; we met a real need. As time has gone by, more and more colleges and universities have begun to offer a program similar to ours.

While they have not had the success of our program, the added competition has made our recruiting more difficult. We strive to show how our program is the best option. To this end, we showcase the relationships the students form while learning side by side, the successes of former students, and the relationships with the instructors.

College and university programs at the graduate level have become readily available from online institutions. Online institutions look very convenient, but often their students have problems with state regulations not being current. Also, students may have little or no interaction with other students or professors. One of the most important desires graduate students mention is to have discussions and interactions with other students and instructors. This information has become important to consider as our university joins the online program delivery model.

Due to the COVID-19 pandemic our university had to quickly develop ways to deliver our programs while under a lockdown situation. Since both students and instructors were unable to meet face to face, it was mandated for all graduate programs to be offered online. At the start of the pandemic, we needed to be certain our classes could continue. Instructors taught mainly through the Zoom platform. We were able to meet the needs of the students and complete that semester's courses with few issues. Those of us who work in graduate enrollment realized we needed to look toward the future and plan for the unknown.

After surveying our current graduate students to find out if they preferred online learning or face-to-face learning, we were a bit surprised by the results. While there were a few students who love face-to-face classes and want nothing to do with online learning, the majority favored moving toward the online format. During the pandemic, health issues as well as course content needed to be considered. There are many options available to students, and for our institution to stay current we needed to join the online movement.

After much deliberation and discussion, our university decided to deliver all graduate programs online moving forward. As an Admissions officer this threw up some red flags. How would we recruit for a totally online program? What would be our talking points since our well-regarded face-to-face program would no longer exist? And most importantly, will students still apply?

As scary as stepping off a cliff into the unknown, we in Admissions were stepping into an arena which was completely new to us. We needed to try new ideas. Our first step was to make greater use of our online/social media presence to announce new programs and other information online, where it can be easily found by graduate prospects, applicants, and students.

Changing to having only an online graduate program will impact our university in many ways. Allowing students to enroll and attend our classes from all areas of this state and other states may affect our enrollment numbers. Our enrollment has been limited by the reach of our cohorts, and of the size of the main university campus that is located in a small town. Our second campus is located in the same city as a large state university.

It is also a very small campus. By having the opportunity to enroll students from any geographic location, we may draw a more diverse student group. This change may be a selling point for our programs. Even though our programs are online, the interaction between students and professors will remain very important. Students are not just a number at our university; we expect our professors to develop a relationship with each student so all of the students will feel comfortable to ask questions or seek advice.

While our off-campus programs have been very successful in bringing in new applicants, recruiting for our main campuses has proven more difficult. Our main campus, located in a small rural community, is where our undergraduate student population resides. These students, who are already engaged with the university and its activities, provide Graduate Admissions with a pool of possible applicants.

As noted earlier, surveys from our current students, both graduate and undergraduate, and target groups, provided valuable information allowing us to develop programs needed and desired. One such program is our new graduate degree in counseling. Another program developed because of survey information was a certificate in Business.

Our MBA program, which is offered on both campuses, must compete with the program offered by a large state university. Each year the dean of our School of Business questions us as to how can we make our program stand out from the competition. The answer changes year to year, as it reflects the changing trends in business. One major advantage we discovered is that we offer our degree in the evenings where our competition does not.

It is very easy to saturate a market when the market area is small. We hope opening our programs to anyone interested across the state, nation, or other countries will positively impact our graduate enrollment. With an additional admissions staff member dedicated to recruiting applicants from out of state, overseas, and even the military, the potential market increases exponentially. These are opportunities we have not had before, and we plan to take advantage of them.

Many individuals are looking for ways to improve their qualifications for future employment or advancement in their present job. This could be accomplished for both the fields of Education and Business via certificate programs. While the students would not earn a degree, they would earn a certificate attesting to gained knowledge and skills that should benefit their current and future positions. Career job enhancement is the main reason people return for a graduate degree.

Advertising the value of postgraduate studies, either degree or certificate programs, featuring the benefits to be gained is likely to capture the attention of prospective applicants. If we can show positive examples of these benefits, then individuals may see how the programs might benefit them personally. Then, we are much more likely to enroll them in our programs.

Graduate enrollment is projected to grow incrementally over the next 8–10 years. The only way to be part of this growth is to keep ahead of trends, meet the needs of applicants and students, and recruit where there are opportunities. It takes a strong team to do this work. Adding another Graduate Admissions staff member to the team would create many more recruiting opportunities. Currently, our small staff is limited in the amount we can do. There are possibilities we cannot pursue, as all of our time is already allocated. It's amazing how well our team succeeds each semester by recruiting more than our set goals.

Fortunately, retention is not an issue at our university. At most colleges and universities, the recruiting, advising, and retention roles are managed by different offices. At our university all of these tasks are managed by one office—the Office of Graduate Studies, which is part of the Office of Graduate Admissions. Once our graduate students make the decision to enter graduate school, they stay.

If a student does leave, the main reason is due to life issues. We have no control over these concerns. The Admissions office provides all graduate students guidance, advising support, and mentoring. We offer conflict resolution if needed. Recruiting a diverse, capable, and engaging population of graduate students is only realistic if the recruiters understand the student population.

The personal touch is what matters in today's fast-paced, revenue-based university setting. We in Admissions should never lose sight of this. We must all work to foster an environment where learning and growing is as important as the number of students enrolled. Our strong retention rates show the success of all offices working together to provide a personalized experience for each customer—our graduate student and, ultimately, their employers.

The future of Graduate Admissions is dependent on the ability of the staff and faculty to move into the digital age of recruiting and teaching. We must understand how to use all forms of media to make showcasing our university interesting during virtual admissions tours and to have engaging virtual and online learning take place. There will be the need for more live online question and answer sessions. We need to show prospective students what our university offers, but also allow them to see themselves as part of the experience. This will attract future learners to our programs.

Moving to a completely online environment will mean there will be the need for additional services to support our students and for them to stay connected to the college. For example, adult students will need assistance with technology, perhaps tutoring and counseling, and financial aid—all from a distance. We must ensure we offer the certificates and other opportunities for students who only require gaining or updating their precise skillset. Working as a team is essential. We must all work as a team, looking toward the future, providing new programs, ideas, and opportunities so our institution does not stagnate—so that it can continue to move forward.

CODA—PERRY RETTIG

There are other strategies that may be considered in order to recruit undergraduate students, particularly those student groups which exist in robust numbers—underrepresented populations and nontraditional-aged students.

When Perry Rettig was a K-12 public school principal, he had served at schools with significant Hispanic and Southeast Asian student populations. He was concerned, however, these students did not have any teachers from their same backgrounds. So, he visited with the president at then Lakeland College and they began the Urban Teacher Outreach Program, or UTOP. The UTOP was designed to recruit Southeast Asian and Hispanic paraprofessionals from the two local school districts in order for them to return to college on weekends, evenings, and summers and earn their college degrees and teacher certifications.

The original cohort began with twenty-five students. Tuition was paid entirely through Pell Grants and the Lakeland College endowment. The school districts supported these students through mentorships, student-teaching experiences, and interviews for teaching vacancies when they completed their studies. In turn, this program brought new underrepresented populations to the college. Many of these students have gone on to teach in the region, while others might have ultimately changed majors but are now working in professional fields nearby. Their children have often now gone onto college and have found success within the community.

Another program, focusing on nontraditional-aged students, occurred years later when Rettig served as Associate Vice Chancellor for Academic Affairs at the University of Wisconsin Oshkosh. The ANSR (Adult Nontraditional Student Resources) Office was created to reach out to area adult students who were not currently attending college, but who had earned some college credits from the university before they "stopped out."

The very small staff in the ANSR office reached out to these individuals to discuss how close they were to completing an associate or bachelor's degree. For example, some students had stopped out, but had already earned enough credits for an associate's degree. By completing the appropriate paperwork, they could immediately earn a degree credential. Some of these students would then continue on to finish a bachelor's degree which now seemed to be within striking distance.

Other students only needed to take somewhere between three and twelve credits to earn a bachelor's degree. The ANSR staff put together sample course loads for these students so that they could complete their degrees in one or two semesters. These students were also told the amount of their tuition bills, as well as their financial aid packages. Again, just a little extra assistance or incentives made a huge difference for these working adults. Some only needed an inducement of a $250 scholarship to help them complete their degrees. Immediately these students were able to move up in their organizations or seek better employment elsewhere.

In the previous essay, Kathleen Carter mentioned how she and her colleagues have worked with local school districts to create cohort programs for teachers to earn advanced degrees. These students could take graduate courses at their own school sites—college professors and adjunct instructors from the local districts would go to them.

This model could easily be replicated through partnerships with local businesses. For example, should a business be able to secure a critical mass of employees (perhaps as little as ten) who need to take additional coursework to complete an associate or bachelor's degree, the university could have their professors work on-site teaching the necessary courses. The professors would teach their requisite coursework, but student papers and projects could focus on the needs of the business. Everyone wins in such an arrangement, and better partnerships would follow. In fact, with a sufficient number of guaranteed students in the program, a special pricing arrangement could be made.

NOTES

1. Josh Miller. "10 Things You Need to Know about Gen Z." *HR Magazine.* SHRM.org. October 30, 2018.

2. Karen Doss Bowman. "Shifting Demographics." *Trusteeship:* Association of Governing Boards of Universities and Colleges. (March/April, 2020) 28(2): 22.

3. Laura Hamilton, Josipa Roksa, and Kelly Nielsen., "Providing a 'Leg up': Parental Involvement and Opportunity Hoarding in College," SAGE: American Sociological Association, 2018 *91*(2): 119. Journals.sagepub.com/home/soe.

4. Genevieve Shaw Brown. "After Gen Z, Meet Gen Alpha: What to Know about the Generation Born 2010 to Today." Interview on goodmorningamerica.com. February 17, 2020.

5. Ibid. Miller.

Miller explains, though, that students still prefer face-to-face communication (43%), compared to 24 percent who prefer text messaging, and 14 percent who prefer email.

6. Ian Wilhelm. "New Models for Assessing Applicants." *The Chronicle of Higher Education*. April 30, 2020, 2–3.

7. Ibid. Hamilton et al.

8. Emsi. Emsi Q4 2019 Data Set. www.economicmodeling.com.

9. Jaleesa Bustamante. "College Enrollment & Student Demographic Studies." *Educationdata.org*. https://educationdata.org/college-enrollment-statistics/. June 7, 2019.

Chapter 3

Student Success and Retention

INTRODUCTION

Perhaps the place where enrollment management can make the biggest difference is in the area of student retention and persistence toward graduation. National statistics indicate student retention rates are 67 percent, while graduation rates are 44 percent.[1] No campus leader could be satisfied with these results. "Grawe cites data from the National Student Clearinghouse Research Center estimating that just 62 percent of the students who started college in 2017 returned to the same institution next fall."[2] It should be noted that national retention data are reported for full-time freshmen to sophomore year cohorts, and graduation data are recorded, not after four years, but rather after six years.

Enrollment management requires collaboration and accountability. While every employee is responsible for student recruitment and student success—shown through retention, persistence, and graduation—formal leaders and groups must be assigned ultimate authority for these results. "Collaboration in multiple situations that begins with early engagement among individuals in teams across organizational boundaries achieves outcomes that meet organizational needs as well as individual and team objectives."[3] Such formal roles and responsibilities will be the focus of chapter 5.

The approach to student success and retention is complex, and successful strategies must be comprehensive and given time to take root. To isolate a particular program or initiative to student success is pure folly. This and the remaining chapters will provide clear examples of strategies that have worked but always as part of an interconnected robust plan. Efforts supporting low-income students, students of color, first-generation students, and transfer students are good places to start, as well as a purposeful focus on college transition, tutoring, counseling, and career services.

Ruffalo Noel Levitz ranked a number of retention strategies in terms of their effectiveness. In order, the highest ranking are academic support (tutoring), professional advising, practical work experiences (internships and experiential learning), first-year experience courses, and early career services programs. The same research showed effectiveness rates for programs designed for particular student populations: programs for first-year students, honors programs for advanced students, programs for adult/nontraditional students, and programs for veterans.[4]

In chapter 4, Tingle and Schmitz will discuss tremendous results in student retention vis-à-vis High Impact Practices (HIPs) at Piedmont University. Their college-wide endeavors were based on the research of George Kuh and sponsored by the American Association of Colleges and Universities.[5] Not only do all students reap the benefits of HIPs in terms of retention, but students of color see even more significant gains.[6] Further, not only does participation in HIPs increase retention rates, but it also reduces the time it takes for students to attain their college degrees.[7]

The three essays to follow will provide real-life examples of retention efforts from individuals involved in two disparate regions of the country—the Southeast and the Midwest, as well as on different types of college campuses—a small, private liberal arts university, and a mid-sized, public comprehensive university. In addition, there will be initiatives described at a state-wide university system. Cat Wiles and Perry Rettig will share current efforts at Piedmont University in northeast Georgia. They will describe an innovative team called "the Retention Vortex" and their use of student data and an internal enterprise communication system.

Jenni Walsh will share examples from both a state university approach and from a state university system approach in Wisconsin. The innovations in her discussion will have broad application to general student populations but will even have a more particular focus on underrepresented student groups. Petra Roter will likewise speak from both a state university and a state system perspective, but the innovations and philosophical approaches she will share come from a different vantage point—that of a senior administrative leader.

ESSAY: CAT WILES AND PERRY RETTIG— THE STUDENT RETENTION VORTEX

While our university had seen continued growth of incoming students, both First Time in College (FTIC) and Transfers, the retention rates for these same student populations from freshmen to sophomore year continued to decline at a corresponding rate. In fact, each subsequent year set a record for new enrollments surpassing the previous year's record. The same could be said in student housing. However, losing nearly as many students as we had gained was both disappointing and frustrating. These problems were even worse at the satellite campus one hour away.

The standard retention approaches that had worked in the past were no longer effective. Gone were the days where typical hard work by Admissions officers brought in steady and sufficient enrollments. The college president wanted to increase undergraduate enrollments to a sustainable level of 1,000 residential students. The headcount was closer to 500 at the time. An interesting aside—roughly 60 percent of the total Full-Time Equivalent (FTE) students occupied graduate programs, primarily through teacher education programming at the master's, specialist, and doctoral degrees. Only 40 percent of the total FTE came from undergraduate students. The president called for these percentages to be flipped.

At the time, the university had not designated a formal position to oversee enrollment management. The vice president for Academic Affairs served as de facto enrollment officer, as well as supervisor of Student Affairs. Enrollment figures were trending in the wrong direction, so the VPAA convened an Enrollment Management Task Force. This team chaired by the VPAA consisted of faculty representatives from each of the four schools, and directors from the offices of Undergraduate and Graduate Admissions, Financial Aid, the Registrar, and Student Affairs.

After a year of SWOT analysis, data analysis, and debate, the task force decided the urgent focus must be on student retention. Several initiatives were developed. First, the Division of Student Affairs needed an overhaul. [This initiative will be covered in the following essays]. Over the next couple of years, new student services staff were hired, as the dean of students also served as the sole employee in both Career Services and the Counseling Center. Therefore, a new director was hired for both the offices of Career Services and the Counseling Center. This was followed by subsequent hiring of a director of Tutoring Services, and later by a coordinator of Experiential Learning.

After these student retention efforts were put into place, the VPAA created a Retention Vortex. This group, made up of a subset of individuals from the Enrollment Management Task Force, had two primary functions. The first function related to an examination of policies, procedures, and internal communication patterns that might inhibit student retention. For example, it was learned that Student Accounts Payable and Financial Aid messaging were in conflict with one another and the timing of communications did not flow well for families. Similarly, messaging from Admissions and Residence Life were at times in conflict with one another causing confusion for families and made internal data analysis incomprehensible.

Therefore, communication across the silos was critical, and tremendous improvement has been made. This original intent of the Retention Vortex remains, as it continues to examine workflow, communication messaging and timing, and has far better data integrity. Families have benefited, and professional staff no longer make adjustments or communications without consulting with other offices across divisions. Finally, an examination of retention data along with anecdotal observations by staff help the Vortex to develop and implement new strategies to support students persist toward graduation. The adoption of an early alert system, and a student retention management system are two prime examples.

The Retention Vortex has a rhythm to its operations throughout each semester. At the beginning and middle portion of each semester it carries out the functions elucidated above. However, at the point in the semester where students begin to register for the following semester courses, the Retention Vortex group shifts its focus entirely. The following pages describe this intense work and team effort.

This Vortex group began as an idea to find a way to increase student retention. With an excel spreadsheet and at a conference table the idea formed of assembling a team of people with the goal of keeping students on track to graduate. We needed a variety of partners from all areas of the university to participate. What would it look like? How often would it meet? Who would be the most responsible partners involved? How receptive would faculty be? How would we contact students? So many questions came to mind.

This group evolves every year. We find new ways to make it more efficient and effective, and in doing so we have shown to have better retention numbers year after year. A little effort along the way has shown us the great result at the end of every semester. The idea of just a little more money would allow us to totally focus our attention on this issue year-round instead of only at registration time.

How did we start?

The vice president of Enrollment Management created the original team of ten to twelve people from across the university. Jump to 2020 and we have around fifteen faculty and staff members from many areas (Residential Life, Student Success, Faculty, Admissions, Administrative Assistants, Athletics, Registrar, and the Business office). As a side note, this group originally started with department heads but has gradually spread down the organizational chart to get a good cross section of employees.

These people all have different perspectives on why a student may or may not return. The Vortex excel spreadsheet became the holy grail that this group worked from; it is stored on a shared drive so that team members may access it on a daily basis. The spreadsheet is updated each morning by the Registrar's Office with different codes (Y = registered, blank = we do not know the student status, NR = not returning, GONE = left without talking to anyone, etc.). The Total Withdrawal Form (TWF), completed by the student, is a critical document used on campus to give an idea as to why a student was leaving. One Vortex member has the responsibility of updating the spreadsheet with this information daily.

The TWF tells us the reason the student gave as to why they left, and if they transferred, where to? Were they unhappy with their dorm, or was there financial issues blocking them from returning? All this information is collected and placed on this single spreadsheet, and every week the Vortex team meets to discuss who has not registered and what they know might be going on. The spreadsheet can be sorted by campus, class rank, gender, athletes, advisor, GPA, Business office financial hold, etc. With this information we can use pivot tables to give the team a quick look at the percentage of students registered or not registered every day in any category.

Starting the week after registration opens, we meet for an hour and review the list and watch the numbers. Everyday these numbers will change. It will be a slow and tedious process at first and nearing the deadline for registration the numbers will grow at a more rapid pace. As we get further into registration, we start assigning Vortex team members to students with whom they might have a personal relationship. For example, the coach in our group will tackle the athletes and start reaching out to them to remind them to register or to learn of difficulties. A contact person at our second campus location will start reaching out to students who attend there.

They then will come back and make notes of their findings on the spreadsheet. As each team member reaches out, we find that sometimes students just needed the reminder. We also find that maybe a form has not been turned into the Registrar or the student has not been able to reach the advisor and needs a little extra assistance making that connection. We are the liaison trying to help that student return to our university.

In 2019 the university adopted a virtual student success platform. It would connect students to advisors, instructors, tutors, counselors, and residential life staff to empower these students to reach out and make contact with these university partners. The Vortex could use the program to see the notes faculty might have added on the student or the grades the student was receiving to determine if he or she needed help and where.

The faculty are able to raise flags and send a student to tutoring or counseling, if needed. They can also send notes directly to students to encourage with a positive message or to remind them that they need to register for classes. This tool has been transformative to our university. The Student Success Center (SSC) can use this program to schedule appointments, make notes about a student, and to track a student's engagement with them.

This tool, like the Vortex, will take a couple of years to reach its full potential. Launching this next semester, we will have the ability to input our data and see how any particular student would score on a retention scale. Instead of us manually looking for a student, it will give us a list that we can now work from to prioritize those needier students. We can also see data trends on students we have admitted in order to gain a better understanding of the type of student we need to admit that will more likely succeed.

The data will also allow the university to see the time and date appointments are being booked in the Student Success Center (Counseling, Tutoring, Career Services), and will allow us to increase the hours where we need more support available. It also will allow the university to see if students are taking advantage of services offered, such as the Career Center. So much more information at our fingertips allows for better customer support from the institution.

Another new feature is the ability to have a student let their advisor know if they have a scheduling concern with their classes. The university also created an incoming freshmen checklist that gives students the ability to see what information they must provide to the university. This checklist includes items from Admissions and Residence Life, online orientations they must attend, or immunization forms or surveys that need to be filled out. Wrapping this extra layer of support around the students can only benefit our already ongoing retention efforts.

To provide this service the university needed a lead for the project; so the dean of students was selected. Who better to know what is happening with student success and how the university reaches out to a student than her? We also needed two IT people to be able to extract all of the data (six years' worth) and be able to connect it to the new student success platform. A faculty member showed interest in the project and an administrative assistant from the Enrollment Management team was chosen to keep everyone on task. This core group would bring in others across campus routinely to gain advice on how this software could assist their departments.

With more information at our fingertips the university has been better able to analyze our data and address many different individual needs. Faculty, through this new platform, have been able to become included in the retention process. Flags can be created to note if a student is not responding to registration, and flags can be automatically raised if a student earns a D/F grade, for example.

Flags were also created to determine who needs to know if a student is not comporting themselves well in class, and to ask if a student is having learning difficulties due to COVID-related issues. Now we can communicate among the campus partners that are associated with any student about the real needs that student is having. Using this tool gave us the ability to expand from fifteen people on the Vortex team to the entire university faculty and staff being able to give input to the most appropriate areas on campus that can reach out and help. As a result, our retention numbers have dramatically improved.

Looking forward to a next step in this process, with a little supplemental funding, we could offer a small emergency financial aid grant to help the student who needed only a small amount to be able to register. We could also boost our Counseling and Wellness support services across campus. We could look at the students who dropped out with only a few classes to go and try to recruit them back to finish—a re-entry plan, if you will.

An easy step would be to make it a mandatory process that students must fill out a Total Withdrawal Form before exiting the college so that the university could have a more robust understanding of the reasons students are leaving. The next major step would be hiring a retention coordinator to work on issues year round instead of only working on retention when it is time to register for classes.

Conclusion. Prior to the creation of the Enrollment Management Task Force and the Retention Vortex, the college saw its freshmen to sophomore retention rates spiral downward. The final three years went from 68 percent down to 65 percent and finally to 62 percent. Since then, this number has begun to rebound to 66 percent and most recently to 77 percent in the fall 2020.

A former Botany professor once drew a parallel to transplanting shrubs. He said, "The first year the plant sleeps. The second year the plant creeps. The third year the plant leaps." Indeed, these combined efforts have taken a great deal of planning and development. Success has taken time, but the rewards are only now beginning to come in. A vision, focus, hard work, persistence, and dedication from the team make the difference.

ESSAY: JENNI WALSH—USING HIGH IMPACT PRACTICES IN STUDENT AFFAIRS

Today's colleges realize the co-equal status of the divisions of Student Affairs with Academic Affairs. The total student experience cannot exist without this deliberative collaboration. We should care about all students' grades, how they are balancing school and life, and what goes on outside the invisible fence of higher education. As educators, we need to move beyond the traditional teaching/learning paradigm. We are all accountable and expected to care about the whole student, not only for strategic enrollment purposes, but because it is the right way to educate future community and corporate leaders.

First-generation students are concerned with how to afford college, rarely have savings or other financial support mechanisms in place, and balance the delicate world of going to school full time. They are primarily focused on their career path and not as interested in cocurricular activities unless they are linked to potential career opportunities. Today's college students expect universities to prepare them for their careers and demand that we stick to the script. They come in focused on career exploration and want to leave our universities prepared for future leadership and career opportunities.

For staff in the divisions of Student Affairs, much of the philosophical foundation for student success and retention comes from the work of George Kuh and his HIPs.[8] These researched endeavors have been highly tested and adopted by the many universities across the country as best practices in increasing rates of student retention and engagement among students from a variety of backgrounds. These HIPs have a decided focus on hands-on career preparedness, leadership development, and thinking comprehensively about complex issues.

Practices that we implemented include First Year Seminar, Common Intellectual Experiences, Undergraduate Research, Diversity/Global Learning, Service-Learning/Community-Based Learning, and Internships. Other HIPs include Learning Communities, Writing-Intensive Courses, Collaborative Assignments and Projects, ePortfolios, and Capstone Courses and Projects.

Several of these HIPs have been featured at the University of Wisconsin Baraboo Sauk County.

1. First Year Seminars: At this small liberal arts two-year campus, all students were required to enroll in a freshman-level first-year seminar course. This class provides a critical opportunity for all students to learn the foundational components of higher education. The seminar is a great opportunity for all students to gather the same information that will help them be successful at the collegiate level. Course topics range from basic educational skills such as test taking, studying skills, and time management to diversity, importance of the liberal arts, and undergraduate research options.
2. Internships: Internships are a terrific way for college students to learn the soft skills needed in the workforce, technical skills needed for various careers, and connections to future opportunities. For instance, a local hospital Human Resource Department accepted one of our students in a bachelor's degree completion program. During the end of semester evaluation, the student's supervisor—who was the vice president of Human

Resources—was asked if, given the opportunity, would she hire this student. She responded that yes, she was interested in hiring the student and they currently had a human resources generalist position available.

She went on to state that if this student hadn't done an internship within her department, she would have never considered her. Instead, she often hired graduates from a larger research-based higher education institution in the area. The student was able to showcase her talents while gaining valuable skills in the human resources field, which set her apart from other candidates and gained her a fulfilling career.

3. Service-Learning/Community-Based Learning: As we know, there are a variety of ways that we learn. One of the most effective ways of learning is by completing a hands-on experience and then teaching this skill to others, as Edward Dale's Learning Pyramid exhibits below (see Figure 3.1).[9] Service learning, or community-based learning, is a teaching methodology that directly ties a community-based experience with the learning objectives of the course. It is directly tied to the course curriculum and is not a cocurricular volunteer experience. Additionally, these opportunities tie directly into Generation Z students' interests in treating people with respect, voluntary service, and giving back to their communities.

Examples of effective service-learning/community-based learning include coordinating placements for gerontology students to assist Hmong elders in learning basic English skills; linking students in a health and nutrition class with Boys and Girls Club members to teach the younger students about concepts related to their course content and opportunities to make healthy snacks; requiring all students who take an Introduction to Multicultural American class to have a service-learning experience working with a population that they were unfamiliar with; and, having chemistry students work alongside local cemetery staff to clean headstones that had been affected by oxidation, hydrolysis, and carbonation.

Other retention strategies within Student Services consist of data collection and analysis. Early Alert processes allow faculty members to submit academic or attendance delinquencies. Student Service staff then follow up with these students to let them know that they are a valued member of the campus community and find out if there is any assistance that the university can provide to them.

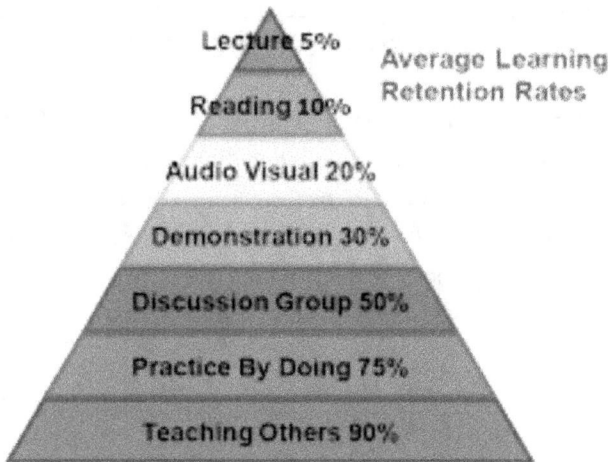

Figure 3.1 Dale Learning Pyramid.

Another example of data collection is a database of student advising appointments. Staff take detailed notes in order to best serve students and get to know more about their particular circumstances. This allows staff/student relationships to move beyond a foundational level and provides an opportunity for staff to recall various details about students.

The final retention strategy that has been quite successful is academic coaching. This is a program that helps students organize and stay focused on their academic work. Student Service staff participate in formal training and students are either recommended by a faculty member or a Student Service staff member. Students meet with their academic coach at least once per week.

We were able to obtain some funding from the University Foundation so that students who were successful in the program, by achieving a grade point average of 2.0 or better, were awarded academic scholarships for the next semester. Students were quite eager when they found out that they would be eligible for an academic scholarship. It was a big honor and boosted their confidence knowing that they were achieving academic success.

While the demographics of today's college students have changed quite dramatically, Student Services professionals must continue to explore researched and proven methods on how to effectively assist students in their pursuit of academic and cocurricular experiences that lead to meaningful career and leadership opportunities in their communities. Working in collaboration with faculty, success stories are being written every day.

ESSAY: PETRA ROTER—STUDENT AFFAIRS— THE VIEW FROM 30,000 FEET

The life and function of a Senior Student Affairs Officer (SSAO) seems to be one of the great mysteries of higher education and is often misunderstood. Student Affairs has been described as the "other side of the house" with the house being the university. It was made to sound like it was that side of the house where the laundry room or mud room were. It was the side of the house that was lived in and served great purpose but far away from the great room that visitors see.

Part of the issue is that each university has structured its Student Affairs division differently. No SSAO has the exact same portfolio of programs, services, and responsibilities as other SSAOs. Portfolios are like snowflakes. Such varied portfolios might include:

Assessment, Advising, Admissions and overall Enrollment Management, Campus Ministers, Campus Safety and Police, Crisis Management, Career Services, Commuter Student Programs, Dean of Students, Discipline and Judicial Affairs aka Conduct, Fraternities and Sororities, Housing, Dining, Health Center, Counseling Center, Disabilities and Accessibility, Leadership Programs, Multicultural Student Programs and Centers, New Student Orientation, Parents Programs, Service Learning and Volunteerism, Recreation and Fitness, Student Activities/Organizations, Student Governance, College Union, Child Care Center, Registrar's Office, Intercollegiate Athletics, Compliance (Clery and Title IX), and even University Parking.

An elevator speech might be, "I help provide the resources, environment, programs, and services that support and advance the learning that takes place in and outside the classroom and lead to success for all students." People would nod but still not fully understand, because that would only scratch the surface. Further, the SSAO is a senior administrator and leader who is responsible to the University, and President or Chancellor. They are an advisor to and a voice for the Chief Executive Officer. This also includes service to communities and states, and at times, university systems.

The job is about developing a collaborative and open relationship with the provost and faculty, and making the house one big open concept house where students can take advantage of all it has to offer. It is working as a team member and leader on the cabinet and partner with colleagues to advance and realize a clear mission and vision. It is being able to collaborate, facilitate, innovate, and be responsive to student and campus needs for the immediate and long term.

The SSAO advocates for and carries the student voice to places that did not have students at the table. The SSAO represents and champions the campus and students to business and community leaders to help build networks and collaborations that benefit the students and fosters the proposition of a university as a public good. We tell and share the stories of good works and deeds.

The Student Affairs leader must develop an extraordinary business acumen and be an outstanding fiscal steward. They must be a friend and fund raiser for programs, scholarships, and the university. Another skillset in this administrator role is in the area of facilities—designing, building, renovating, repairing, and maintaining. This is necessary to meet the ever-changing needs of students and provide environments and spaces for them to learn, grow, and develop.

Student Affairs professionals have been focused and dedicated to student success long before student success became the buzz word of the past few decades. We have long been in a position to provide those experiences, programs, and services that support all our students through all the stages of their education journey. We have been holistic and intentional and have worked to give meaning to student learning and development. We have believed in and advanced the empowerment and engagement of students, including our underrepresented and disenfranchised students, as well.

We have always been about "high impact" practices—a concept that originated from Student Affairs programs—and aligning with the learning outcomes established by the institution and Academic Affairs. Even more, early Student Affairs administrators were charged with the character development of their students.

Over the past few decades there has been an increased emphasis on compliance, accountability, and responsibilities that have placed a greater emphasis on student conduct, community expectations, and ethical and character development. We continue to provide character development through work with students in the areas of civic engagement, volunteerism/service learning, and social justice, and developing future leaders and change agents.

It should also be known that student affairs is a field of scholarly knowledge and practice. The vast majority of SSAOs are academically prepared and most possess doctorates or advanced degrees. Most have taught in the classroom, and thus, understand the central academic and educational missions of the institution.

We are versed in assessment and evaluation, as we know in these fiscally constrained days, we need to provide data as to how programs and services are value-added and advance the mission. We use assessment and data to ensure our programs and services are effective, relevant, and meet the needs of our students. The data also helps us to ensure we are not inadvertently constructing roadblocks and hurdles to student success and allows us to dismantle the ones we discover.

Both the times and our students are changing. We understand those realties and look ahead to issues we need to continue to address. A good SSAO takes time from putting out the fires of the day and strategically looks to the future for change. They are versed in best practices and implementation of those programs. Challenges, which we can also call opportunities, are many on the student success front. These are the things that keep us up at nights. A few of these are:

- The complex and increasing mental health issues of our students—Many students are not able to access the care and programs they need on campus or in our communities. Students are reporting significantly more stress, depression, anxiety, and sleep disorders. Identifying and working with students who are at risk of harm to themselves and others is crucial. Providing environments and programs that address mental health issues improves learning and success and is also preventative in nature.
- Parental involvement—Each year staff find themselves spending more and more time with parents and on parent calls. These parents are known as: helicopter parents, dry cleaner parents, and snowplow parents. They are more demanding than ever before, and they want to be directly involved in their son's and daughter's lives. All need time and attention and coaching on parenting a college student. It provides opportunities to engage parents as part of our communities and to extend campus boundaries.
- Alcohol and other drugs—Alcohol has been a perennial problem on college campuses but now students are coming to campuses with established patterns of alcohol use and abuse, and drug usage is increasing among students. We are seeing many more students who are victims of the opiate epidemic.

- Health and safety—Prevention and education on campus violence, sexual assault, and bias and hate crimes are of constant concern. Providing advocacy and being able to mobilize resources in a timely and responsive manner take much of our attention, along with responding to contagious disease incidents, epidemics, and crisis situations.
- Access and affordability—Increased costs of attendance with dwindling resources and financial aid is leading to greater student anxiety, homelessness, hunger, crippling student loan debt, and stopping or dropping out.
- Diversity and inclusion—Universities are the places where our future leaders are born and developed. It is our responsibility to ensure they are engaged and understand social justice, equity, global citizenship, and inclusion. It is also the place where we can learn to understand and address the "isms" in our world and communities. Campus climate needs to be open, civil, and welcoming to ensure student success.

There are many things that keep the SSAO up at night. One of these are the Student Affairs division staff who do extraordinary work with students at all hours, weekends, and holidays. It is important to know Student Affairs is not 9–5 Monday–Friday, because that is not how our students operate. SSAOs and Student Affairs directors worry about staff stress levels and work-life balance. They worry about doing more with less. Leaders worry what another budgetary cut would mean for a budget that was around 87 percent personnel. At times we have needed to non-renew staff, lay staff off, not replace vacant positions, and we know those vacant positions are never convenient or strategic.

If asked what we would do with an extra $10,000 dollars, the first thing we would do is thank you profusely. Then we would ask a question that may make us look like ingrates, "Is that base-dollars or one-time dollars?" There never has been a SSAO who would turn down money either way. An extra base allotment would likely be put into staff—part-time counselor, advisor, advocate, admission's counselor, or make one of those already on staff a full FTE.

One-time dollars would go into programming or programming supplies like a speaker on diversity, new computers for a student lab, safety equipment for the police, training for staff who are responsible for compliance reporting, additional student wage monies for high-impact campus employment.

Supplies, equipment, and training are the first to get cut and have been for years and are essentially nonexistent. So one-time dollars are always appreciated in those areas.

It should be noted and clarified that this is by no means meant to be a woe for us, the poor misunderstood SSAO missive. To use the student vernacular, "it's complicated." You will find that despite the challenges and concerns and issues that an SSAO faces, we will tell you it is the best job ever. It is gratifying to see students grow and develop and do great things on our campuses and in our communities. To watch them become social change agents, volunteers, and leaders in our communities is its own reward. They become supporters of higher education and our campuses. Knowing that we played a role in that makes our hearts sing.

If you ask an SSAO what is their favorite event on campus, they will tell you hands down it is commencement. At commencement, we see our students, their families, and friends celebrating their accomplishments, and we marvel as to how far they have come and how everyone is transformed. We become reenergized and our faith of limitless potential is renewed. We witness the power of education and value of life-long learning. We know that they will go forth and change and contribute to their communities. We know we were an integral part of the success. What other position allows for that kind of impact and reward?

NOTES

1. Compiled from ACT Institutional Data File, 2017. The comparison group is private, four-year institutions offering bachelor's degrees. www.act.org/content/dam/act/unsecured/documents.

2. Doss Bowman, Karen. "Shifting Demographics." *Trusteeship:* Association of Governing Boards of Universities and Colleges. (March/April, 2020), *28*(2): 23.

3. Clayton Smith, Janet Hyde, Tina Falkner, and Christine Kerlin. "The Role of Organizational Change Management in Successful Strategic Enrollment Management Implementation," *Strategic Enrollment Management Quarterly, 8*(2): Summer 2020, 34.

4. Ruffalo Noel-Levitz. "Effective Practices for Student Success, Retention, and Completion Report," 2019.

5. George Kuh. *High Impact Practices: What They Are, Who Has Access to Them, and Why They Matter.* Washington, DC: American Association of Colleges and Universities. 2008.

6. Ashley Finley, and Tia McNair. "Assessing Underserved Students' Engagement in High Impact Practices." Washington, DC: American Association of Colleges and Universities. 2013. https://www.aacu.org/sites/default/files/files/assessinghips/AssessingHIPS_TGGrantReport.pdf

7. Jillian Kinzie. "High Impact Practices: Promoting Participation for All Students." *Diversity & Democracy, 15*(3), 2012: 13–14.

8. George Kuh. "High-Impact Practices: What They Are, Who Has Access to Them, and Why They Matter." Washington, DC: Association of American Colleges and Universities. 2008.

9. Edgar Dale. *Audiovisual Methods in Teaching.* New York: Dryden. 1969.

Chapter 4

The Curricular and the Cocurricular Juxtaposition

While we have the tendency to think of the college student life as two distinctive worlds—the curricular (in class) and the co-curricular (out of class)—nothing could be further from the truth, at least not if we want to consider student success. The co-curriculum and the curriculum are two sides of the same coin, and so they must be considered together. The literature is replete with this evidence.[1] Chapter 4 provides precise examples of this co-equal view and how it blends.

Jeffrey Docking, president of Michigan's Adrian College, explained that in order to grow sufficient student enrollments, institutions of higher learning need to focus on four areas: establish enrollment targets for each academic and athletic program; create new niche academic programs; create new athletic programs; and develop new centers which support the school's mission.[2]

We have already established that today's students expect relevancy and value from their college experiences. They want to earn their way and need each experience to move them toward their goals. For the classroom, it means content that is relevant, contemporary, and interconnected. This does not mean they wish for colleges to dismantle the core of the liberal arts heritage. It is not an either/or proposition; it is a both/and expectation. The academic core is the foundation upon which the major is built. Yet, the content must reach the real-world skills and outcomes employers are seeking.[3]

Perhaps even more crucial is the pedagogy—the way in which professors teach and students learn. Sit and get is gone (never should have been). Teaching and learning are contextual; they must be experiential, problem-based, hands-on, and interconnected.[4] They need to lead to internships, to connections with the cocurricular, and to the community and career.

In a meta-analysis of the literature, Schwieger noted several additional academic strategies that will reach Gen Z students: skills boot camps; alternative credentialing and certifications; research and projects solving employer needs; employer involvement in the curriculum; career development strategies; blended courses; and competitive events.[5] Rhodes explained, "Colleges are moving away from the reductionist dimensions of higher education that arose in the twentieth century to handle expanded access to college to an emphasis on acquiring more of the higher-order skills and abilities necessary for students' health and well-being in life and work."[6]

The essay by Julia Schmitz and Melissa Tingle will share tremendous curricular efforts toward student success. They have taken the research of Kuh and others on High Impact Practices (HIPs) to create transformational experiences both inside and outside the classroom that have led to increases in student retention. With the sponsorship of the American Association of Colleges and Universities, Kuh and his colleagues have identified 11 HIPs: First Year Seminars and Experiences; Common Intellectual Experiences; Learning Communities; Writing Intensive Courses; Collaborative Assignments and Projects; Undergraduate Research; Diversity/Global Learning; ePortfolios; Service Learning, Community-Based Learning; Internships; and Capstone Courses and Projects.[7]

The root to cocurricular is "curricular." The life of the student outside of class must have deep connections to the full experience of today's learners. Besides Kuh's identified HIPs, there are other transformational experiences. Leadership is just such an example. Developing affinity groups is equally critical for today's generation of students. Affinity groups might include student government, campus activities boards, athletic teams, academic clubs and associations, student newspapers, and the list goes on. The research is clear, "Success in college is not just about academics . . . students are more likely to complete college when they are integrated into their campus," as reported by Hamilton and colleagues.[8]

Athletic Director and Coach Jim Peeples pens an essay to follow which describes the impact athletics has played on student-athletes with whom he has worked at several institutions. He further expresses the collaborative efforts he and his colleagues have had across myriad aspects of the university.

Professors Julia Schmitz and Melissa Tingle then explain how Piedmont University has woven HIPs into the curricular and cocurricular fabric of the total student experience resulting in increased retention rates.

Kim Crawford, Emily Pettit, and Perry Rettig, however, begin with an essay articulating the centrality of student leadership training and other experiences which have proven to have a dramatic retention impact at Piedmont University. They further explain the requisite infrastructure necessary to grow and develop a robust Student Affairs division.

ESSAY: EMILY PETTIT, KIM CRAWFORD, AND PERRY RETTIG—STUDENT SERVICES, RESIDENCE LIFE, AND LEADERSHIP

In January of 2014, Piedmont College had a single division of Student Affairs with four professional staff members including the Dean of Students, Director of Student Activities, Director of Fitness and Recreation, and an administrative assistant. At that time, the Dean of Students also served as the Director of Residence Life and the Director of Counseling and Career Services.

The Residence Life department was supported by four live-in graduate assistants (GAs), and approximately 17 undergraduate students serving as resident assistants (RAs). The residence halls housed approximately 450 students. An additional layer of support for student success included the work of faculty members who served in the capacity of Writing Center Coordinator and Tutoring Services Coordinator.

Today, the residence hall population hovers around 750 students, and the halls are at capacity—that's with adding a residential village for upperclassmen. Such growth did not happen organically. Rather, purposeful planning and infrastructure development was required. With the intended increase in residential students, the college needed to fund and support its human capital—essential Student Affairs staff.

While the residential housing numbers were increasing at a rate of 15 percent each year, we found ourselves without the capacity to scale staffing and services as quickly to meet these students' needs. This was not a simple problem of numbers, but it was compounded by the unique needs of Gen Z students for whom we had not yet developed sufficient support services. So, while we were excitedly achieving our goal to increase the residential population, regrettably the college's retention rate decreased during Piedmont's residential student growth. It was clear that the infrastructure for the student support system was not adequate to handle this growth.

In late 2014, the Student Affairs staff of four grew to six professional staff members when we added a Director of Residence Life, and a Counselor. These additional positions were critical first steps to building a Student Affairs division that could support not only the numbers of students but the increasing needs from the Gen Z population.

Between 2015 and 2019 the following positions were added to the Student Affairs staff: Director of Counseling Services, Coordinator of Tutoring Services, Coordinator for Disability Support, Director of Career Services, Student Success Coach, Coordinator for Experiential Learning, Associate Dean of Student Life, Coordinator for Greek Life and Orientation, and two Assistant Directors of Residence Life.

During that same time frame, we boasted three significant facility improvements. A new residential complex was added (adding approximately 150 new beds), a multimillion dollar new Student Commons was also added, and an existing building in the center of campus was named the Student Success Center. In 2019, a count of Student Affairs professional full-time staff numbered a healthy fifteen staff members. Furthermore, the Division of Student Affairs had now developed two distinct arms of support to wrap around our students in our "high touch" campus culture: Student Life and Leadership, and Student Success. This then saw the creation of a new cabinet-level position—Vice President for Enrollment Management and Student Affairs.

This new organizational structure allowed for more discrete operations and reporting lines. Student Success oversees: Counseling, Career Services, Student Success (tutoring services), Accessibility Services, and Experiential Learning. Each of these units now has an office coordinator. Staffing additions in 2020 included two Student Success Advisors. Student Success—headed by an associate vice president—employs 7.5 professional staff.

The subdivision of Student Success saw perhaps the most profound changes of all. Career Services now has a dedicated full-time director with plans for future growth. Hiring an additional staff member in this office is the number one priority for the Vice President of Enrollment Management and Student Affairs. Today's Gen Z students and their parents expect the college experience to prepare them for the professional workforce, and they are looking for universities who show they can do it.

The Counseling Center now has 1.5 professionally licensed and certified staff members and is seeking a post-doc student for additional support. Today's students are needing more counseling services than ever before as the prevalence and acuity mental health needs has surged in the past few years. In an effort to further support the mental health needs of our students, Piedmont has now begun offering three complementary sessions per semester through tele-mental health whereby students select from a national counselor database affording our students access to multilingual counselors, evening and weekend appointments, and psychiatric care.

The Office of Accessibility and Resources (OARS) has seen a significant caseload increase as more and more students enter college with disability support needs. This office was originally staffed by a .25 FTE position housed in Academic Affairs. Due to increased demand in students who need accommodations, this role has become a full-time position and is housed appropriately in Student Success with strong relational ties to Academic Affairs. The increased request for accommodations related to mental health disorders, compounded with the advent of Emotional Support Animals requests, keeps this office extremely busy.

Students registered with the OARS office fell into the following categories: Academic Accommodations (33 students), Attendance Accommodations (8 students), Dietary Accommodations (4 students), and Residential Accommodations including Emotional Support Animals or Service Dogs (13 students). We had one service dog for a residential student and one service dog on the Athens campus.

Students receiving services, fall into the following major categories of disability: Medical (22 students), Learning Disabilities (14 students), ADD/ADHD (9 students), Anxiety/Depression or other Mental Health Concern (17 students), Deaf (1 student), and Autism/Asperger Syndrome (5 students). It is interesting to note that the students with medical eligibility included those with Friedreich's Ataxia, Narcolepsy, Cerebral Palsy, Diabetes, Arthritis, and Migraines, to name a few.

Piedmont's Office of Experiential Learning, otherwise known as Compass, directs student experiential growth opportunities outside the classroom. The program promotes interdisciplinary learning, civic engagement, career development, cultural awareness, and leadership. It helps students to make plans and decisions by working with the broader community. While one documented endeavor is required to graduate, we find some students excitedly complete several experiential endeavors. To recognize these students' advanced achievement, we created an Experiential Learning Honor Society.

Of all the units housed in the Student Success Center, perhaps none has seen more dramatic growth than Tutoring Services. Student usage of this office has grown exponentially, and retention numbers show the results. Gone are the days of students embarrassed to attend one-on-one or group tutoring sessions. They have grown accustomed to such work in their high school experiences. In fact, most athletic coaches require weekly attendance in an academic study hall.

Two major forms of tutoring are available to students. There are the traditional 1:1 sessions where a student seeks the help of another student in a particular subject matter. There are also Supplemental Instruction programs where small groups of students receive extra support from a student tutor. These tutors are identified and recommended by their professors, and then they receive specialized tutoring training. In turn, the tutors work with the professors in order to assist the students with the work currently assigned in the classroom.

Piedmont started a summer bridge (SAIL) program two years ago. This half-week program starts immediately prior to all freshmen move-in. While all new students are invited to attend, those students with lower-than-average high school academic profiles, or those students who are first generation college students, are encouraged to attend. The program takes students off campus for three days for team building and other college prep activities.

All students are paired with an older student mentor, as well as a faculty mentor. Retention rates for these students were significantly higher than the general population. The original cohort of 40 students more than doubled in size to 100 this past year. Ultimately, the goal is to have all freshmen attend the SAIL program.

From strategic planning efforts, another initiative was derived to support student mentoring. The original plan, while not fully funded, called for the hiring of three student success advisors. This first year saw the hiring of two advisors. These recent college graduates mentor a case load of new freshmen students. They help the students navigate the college terrain, provide workshops on such topics as time management, study skills, etc., and they help the students become involved in various affinity groups on campus. For example, they help the students explore HIPs, and various clubs and organizations.

While attending a high touch institution, students expect and are offered personalized support and guidance. To meet these demands, technology has been added to the team as an "invisible" Student Affairs staff member. Scaling services, and strategic and timely campus-wide communication is key to supporting students and retention efforts. In 2019 we added a student success solution platform to our tool belt.

This tool has added an invisible safety net to our student population. It provides a centralized portal for student success and includes all currently enrolled students, their picture, contact information, attributes (e.g., Classification, First Gen, Athlete, Campus location, etc.), major, course grades, and a personalized "success network" of campus partners. In this platform, students, faculty, and staff can collaborate to ensure student progression and success.

Early alerts about student attendance, academic performance, or referrals to counseling and student success advisement have offered an invisible web of support between Student Affairs and Academic Affairs. Without needing to remember the new director's name in the OARS Office, a faculty member can simply send a referral for a student that is automatically routed to the correct professional. That professional reaches out to the student, then closes the loop with the faculty member.

The most recent strategic initiative implemented at Piedmont impacts student diversity recruitment and retention. A campus-wide Council of Diversity, Equity, and Inclusion (DEI) has been initiated with representation of students, faculty, and staff. In addition, a part-time Student Diversity Coordinator is now working as a support system for students. Ultimately, the college plans to make this a full-time position and support faculty and staff recruitment and retention efforts, as well.

While the Division of Student Success has seen dramatic changes, so too has the Division of Residence Life and Leadership. The amount of time students spend inside the classroom each week varies from 15 to 20 hours. So, what do they do for the rest 148–153 hours? Ideally, they are participating in cocurricular activities and programs. Some are involved in student clubs and organizations. Others choose Greek Life or other leadership affinity group opportunities. Institutions of higher education must offer ways for students to invest their time wisely in order to make the most of their college experience.

For a small liberal arts institution who values developing compassionate leaders, we began to explore ways to increase our cocurricular offerings that include opportunities for students to develop their leadership skills and abilities. Part of our institution's mission focuses on developing compassionate leaders and preparing them to serve in the global and local community. As we began to consider ways to provide cocurricular opportunities for students to improve their leadership, we began to reflect on how important it is to help them discover their own leadership abilities.

One way we chose to help students develop their leadership was through offering them the opportunity to take the CliftonStrengths assessment.[9] This assessment is described as a tool for individuals to help them "thrive" everywhere. Rath writes, "Gallup's research has shown how a strengths-based approach improves your confidence, direction, hope and kindness towards others." Therefore, we began to promote and encourage students to take this assessment in order for them to discover more about their leadership capabilities, gain confidence, and ultimately to prepare them to be the leaders of the future.

Once students complete the assessment, they participate in a workshop to discuss their results and how to apply what they learned about themselves. This has allowed students on campus to become aware of their strengths. Not only do they discover their five strengths, but they also learn how they can apply those to leadership opportunities, their majors, and future careers or jobs. In addition, it has started to become a topic of conversation on campus for students to ask what other peers' strengths are.

Furthermore, the leadership workshop and strength discovery has allowed them to find cocurricular activities to get involved in where they can apply those strengths. This has also given us the opportunity to create a culture on campus of awareness and conversation around an individuals' strengths and talents. This past year, students who participated in the assessment and follow-up workshop had a 100 percent retention rate.

While Leadership may not be considered one of George Kuh's High Impact Practices, Piedmont has been able to see the impact that leadership development can have on retaining students. In large part, this is a testament to this generation's desire to have tangible experiences they feel can benefit them. Students that participate are able to see how this experience can benefit them so they can use this information to obtain future career employment opportunities.

To build on the idea of leadership development, a Lions Leaders in Training Institute (LIT) was also created in order to offer consistent training to several student leaders on campus. Essentially, this institute includes a series of hands-on workshops and presentations that cover several areas in leadership. Some of the topics discussed include: Ethics in leadership, Diversity and Inclusion in Leadership, Personal Branding in Leadership, Dealing with Crisis, Professionalism in Leadership, Working as a Team in Leadership, Learning to Listen, and Campus Safety Authority (CSA) training.

Through these trainings, students have been able to explore different areas of leadership and discuss how to directly apply these concepts to their leadership positions on campus. In addition, these topics have allowed for in-depth analysis of how to be a more effective leader. The diversity and inclusion topic alone has equipped leaders to ensure they make students on campus feel safe and supported. Implementing the LIT Institute provided student leaders on campus an opportunity to have difficult conversations around what it means to be a leader.

Another way we have provided leadership pathways for students is through their participation in Greek Life. Several years ago, we began to contact national Greek Life organizations in order to see if any of them would be interested in expanding a chapter to our institution. With the idea of creating affinity groups on campus and future leaders as our focus, we researched organizations that aligned closely with our institution's missions and values. It wasn't long before we were able to identify two that we believed would be a good fit for our campus.

Students were interested in joining these affinity groups so they could meet like-minded individuals with a passion for developing as leaders and serving others. Through these organizations, we have seen students get involved in philanthropic efforts, develop their social and cultural capital, improve academic support, and provide networking opportunities. Each semester, we have seen students that participate in Greek Life have a higher semester average GPA than students who are not members. In fall 2019, Greek members had an average GPA of 3.525 while the all-campus average GPA was 3.17.

Not only is there a difference in their academic performance, but their retention rate is also higher than the institution's average. Greek members were retained from fall 2019 to spring 2020 at a 100 percent retention rate as compared to the institutional average of 91 percent. The retention rate from fall 2018 to fall 2019 was 84 percent for Greek Life participants and 69 percent for the institution. Obviously, the impact that leadership affinity groups have on student persistence and academic progress has been impactful.

In addition to Greek Life, student organizations such as the Student Government Association and the Campus Activities Board provide hands-on approaches to real world scenarios. Students have the opportunity to learn navigating political waters, creating budgets, executing agendas, managing time, planning events, and much more.

These student groups as well as others are part of the cocurricular programming to help enhance the student experience. Their retention rate for student participants was 100 percent from fall 2019 to fall 2020. They see value in the experience they receive from their leadership role. In addition, these positions help students feel a sense of belonging to the institution while also developing relationships with administrators, other departments, as well as peers.

Finally, it must be noted that developing a robust leadership program starts at New Student Orientation. From the time students enter the institution it is imperative that they make a connection right away. At our orientation, we make every effort to be intentional with how we facilitate connections between students. For example, students are assigned a peer mentor that reaches out to them before they even begin attending classes on our campus.

Then, when they arrive at orientation, they have a chance to spend the day with their mentor as well as other peers that share similar interests. This connection with their peer leader is crucial as they begin their journey on campus. This sets the tone for their ability to thrive on campus not only as a student, but as a leader.

Lessons we learned along the way have helped us continue to improve how we serve students. One of the main takeaways from creating a new culture focused on leadership is creating partnerships and pathways with other initiatives and departments on campus. For instance, as part of our Quality Enhancement Plan, we included leadership as a component and an area to focus on. As a result, this helped to secure funding, create buy-in, and identify how other departments could support leadership development in their areas.

Creating partnerships with other departments has been critical to this success. Athletic coaches have hosted leadership workshops. Human Resources has offered to cover the cost of the assessment for employees. In addition, this year, every PDMT 1101 (our freshmen transition course) class has had the opportunity to take the Strengths assessment and attend a follow-up workshop to discuss practical application. It has been through these partnerships that we have truly begun to create a cocurricular pathway focused on developing our students into the leaders that will impact our world.

Creating the infrastructure to help shift the focus from just fun and games to meaningful conversations and growth for our students has taken several years to develop. Each of these areas has helped us to expand our leadership development beyond that of just the strengths assessment and the leadership workshops. What began as an office of four full-time staff members has developed into nine full-time staff members who are focused on developing the whole student as leaders.

Over the past five years, we have converted our five graduate assistant positions to full-time professional staff positions so we have additional support for our students and more touch points outside of their academic faculty. This brought a level of professionalism to the Department of Student Life and Leadership that was missing before, while also offering more quality hours to be spent supporting the student experience.

In addition, we have changed our name from simply Student Activities to Student Life and Leadership. This ensures that we remain true to our core values. With the Dean's ability to focus only on Student Life and Leadership which includes Residence Life, Greek Life, Orientation, Student Activities, Student Clubs and Organizations, Fitness and Recreation, Conduct, the Student Commons, and other student experience areas, it allows for a strong focus on leadership development of the staff as well as the students.

All in all, in order to develop and grow in the area of Student Life and Leadership, institutional leaders must decide what specific mission and values must drive the goals of the department. As such, the focus should remain on the students. It must be a student-centered approach to developing the qualities of each student to support their leadership development and growth. What began for our institution as an idea and something that was in our mission statement has now become an annual focus for the entire department.

It truly takes the efforts of each member to create a culture that is focused on developing leaders that will impact their local and global communities. The cocurricular focus of leadership provides students a way to apply ideals, topics, and theories to hands-on situations. As a result, students are able to hone their leadership skills and directly apply cocurricular concepts, which ultimately prepares them for the next step in their journey.

ESSAY: JIM PEEPLES—ATHLETICS AND LEADERSHIP: RECRUIT WITH RELATIONSHIPS AS THE FOCAL POINT

The athletic recruiting process is critical to achieving overall enrollment goals for many small private liberal arts institutions that are NCAA Division III members. At many of these institutions the number one priority is for the athletic coaching staff to generate new recruits. When large recruiting class size is the focus little to no attention is placed on retention of these new recruits. What occurs in most situations is a number of freshmen to disproportionate upper-class student-athletes. Because of the pressure to recruit with this focus, very little time can be given to truly and honestly getting to know the recruit on a personal level.

The impact of recruiting with this model is very negative for the athletic department and, more globally, the institution. The first impact is usually low freshman to sophomore retention. The next is low overall retention. Because of the impact on retention, the graduation rate also suffers. Typically, these institutions want to grow enrollment, but this creates a cycle of larger numbers in the fall because of the focus on new numbers which then creates smaller numbers in the spring semester.

Then there is little enrollment growth the following semester because retention has suffered. Budgets get cut during the spring and budgets are frozen the following fall. Morale is low and the institution is not growing their enrollment. Finally, every measure that an institution is graded on—freshman to sophomore retention, overall retention, and graduation rates—are all low and the college athletic programs suffer.

In order to grow enrollment through athletics, it is critical for the institution to have a different focus. Athletic teams need to have healthy rosters, not inflated rosters. Attention needs to be placed on retention of student-athletes, rather than on bringing in large classes. Graduating the student-athletes that start in your program is vital to this process. The way this is accomplished is to focus on relationship-building during the recruiting process.

The first step to recruit this way is to recruit student-athletes who are a "good fit" for the institution. A student-athlete must be not only be a good fit in Athletic Department but also in your campus; this needs to be an important consideration during the recruiting process. How is this achieved? It starts by asking the right questions and by being a skillful listener. It has nothing to do with being a great salesperson. What is the critical question? These are things we believe that you need to identify in the beginning of the recruiting process.

Number one, what is the major academic field of study that the prospect is interested in pursuing? Second, what is their preferred learning environment? Next, how far away from home is the student-athlete's comfort zone? Finally, what is the environment directly outside of your campus, and does the student-athlete feel comfortable with the surrounding community? Finding out what a prospect's hobbies and outside interests are is important to discuss. Does your campus or the surrounding community offer those opportunities?

Most of the time student-athletes and their parents have not even considered these questions. They are consumed with thinking about their student-athlete having a spot on the roster, or how quickly will they be starter for that team. It is so important for a coach to remind recruits and their families that everyone will not become a starter. In some cases, they may not get significant playing time on that team. If families are making decisions to attend your institution based on these factors, many times these will not be student-athletes you will retain. Helping the student-athlete and their family chose a school because it is the "right fit" is important to retaining them.

Affordability is another important piece to the puzzle of recruitment and retention of a student-athlete. Arriving at the answer should not be a difficult process to go through with each family. Again, asking the proper questions is what a coach needs to do. Most small private liberal arts institutions have an academic scholarship program that will be determined by the student's GPA, SAT, or ACT test scores, and in some cases the rigor of academic program that was taken. An example would be taking AP courses.

Whatever the criteria that each school uses, it is critical that coaches are well versed in how the academic scholarship will be determined and be able to communicate with the family about that process. A coach should be able to help the family determine an estimate of what the scholarship amount will be. Before the recruiting process goes too far, the coach and the family need to determine what they can afford. If the family indicates that it would be a stretch to afford your school, recruiting them successfully will be a challenge. Retaining that student in the future will be an even greater challenge.

When a family is stretched financially it many times has a negative impact on the student's ability to perform academically as well as athletically. This happens many times with low income families who are Pell eligible. Everyone should have the goal of putting the student in the best position to be successful. When those students have the additional stress of finances, many times their ability to be successful is impacted.

Does the recruit fit your athletic department culture and the culture of the team they want to be on? We have developed a set of "values" for our department. They are tied to the college's "Mission Statement." They are things that each coach should be able to articulate and instill in their student-athletes in their program. They are meant to be tools that each coach can use during the recruiting process to distinguish our department from the competition. To have a strong culture in your department and in each program is critically important to recruit and retain your student-athletes. Those values are things that should be identifiable to a recruit and their family. Because they are tied to the mission of the college, these values should be part of the entire student experience at your institution.

Today, a strong culture will help in the recruiting process, but more importantly, it will help you retain those student-athletes. People will stay at an institution, a job, or on an athletic team if the culture is strong. If the culture is poor, or even worse toxic, recruiting and retaining will be challenging. Culture must be worked on daily, and everyone must be intentional about how they do that. Coaches must daily, by the example they set for their student-athletes, live out those values by being great role models. Culture has nothing to do with words; it has everything to do with action and how people are treated.

It is of the highest importance to make sure during the hiring process for any position in your athletic department that you hire people who understand and embrace your culture. Head coaches, assistant coaches, and support staff who embrace and live the culture of your department are critical. There are outstanding people who work in the field of college athletics, but not all those people will be a good fit for your athletic department. Coaches typically fit into one of two categories: "transformational" or "transactional."

The direction we have been committed to in our department is finding people who are "transformational." It is impossible to have any level of long-term success with coaches who are "transactional" in their approach. Coaches who are truly committed to transforming the lives of the student-athletes they work with have the larger and more important picture in mind. That is the culture we have embraced. That culture cannot be cultivated without having all the right people in place.

If you want to attract quality academic and athletic students, there must be a commitment to excellence and success in the classroom and on the athletic field. It is vitally important to understand that level of commitment needs to hold true for every program in your athletic department. Students who have demonstrated success in high school, in most cases, seek schools where they can continue to be successful in the classroom and be a part of winning athletic programs. Quality people want to be challenged, want to continue growing, and be surrounded by others who share their mindset.

That starts first and foremost at the president and senior administrative level of the college. If the president and upper administration do not believe that achieving success athletically is important, then it does not matter the quality of your coaching and support staff in your athletic department. It takes leaders at the highest level who are willing to support an athletic department with all the resources that are needed to achieve at the highest level.

You must have the ability to hire the best coaches and pay them at a level that is in line with their experience and demonstrated success. Each program needs to have the budget it requires to provide a quality student-athlete experience. The same commitment needs to be there to hire quality support staff in the areas of athletic training, strength and conditioning, and athletic communications. All these pieces are important to having a successful program.

Many people in leadership positions see athletics only through the lens of a revenue stream for the college. They add sports programs just so they can add enrollment numbers but not caring about achieving any level of success. The outstanding presidents care about their athletic programs being successful. Unless you want to be successful in a sport, simply adding athletic programs just for the enrollment numbers will be a losing proposition in the end. Some presidents make the statement that it is about quantity over quality.

Our athletic department is thankful that our president does not share that philosophy. He cares about our student-athletes being successful in all the areas of the life on our campus.

From the fall of 2016 to the fall of 2020 we have grown our student-athlete enrollment by over 130. We have started one new program in the fall of 2019—both a men's and women's swimming program. That program enrolled 25 new freshmen in the fall of 2020. We saw our retention reach an all-time high for the department of 83 percent during this time. There are things we believe we have done extremely well during these past four years that have led to this success.

We award financial aid based on academic merit, and our coaches have done a tremendous job focusing their recruiting efforts on recruiting the highest achieving student-athletes. As an institution we retain these students at over 90 percent. These student-athletes tend be people who are extremely focused and hard working at everything they get involved with on campus. In the fall of 2019, we had over 80 student-athletes achieve a 4.0 GPA and in the spring of 2020 the number was over 90 who achieved that GPA. As a department during these two semesters our combined department GPA in the fall of 2019 was a 3.32, and in the spring of 2020 was 3.42. The commitment to recruiting these types of student-athletes and the culture of excellence are key contributors to our growth. These student-athletes are always the easiest to retain. We have had multiple Academic All-Americans during this time which demonstrates excellence in the classroom and on the fields and courts of play.

The commitment to academic excellence has also gone a long way to developing a great relationship between our faculty and coaches. This relationship, where the lines of communication are always open, helps everyone who has an important connection with a student-athlete to work closely together to support them. A student-athlete's academic success is our department's number one priority. This is evident when you realize that all 19 of our teams achieved over 3.0 GPAs this past year.

During a student-athlete recruiting visit to campus, we begin the process of relationship-building and defining the importance of academics. Every student-athlete meets with a faculty member during their campus visit. Often times, they will meet with the dean of the academic program they are interested in. Many of our coaches will have a current student-athlete from the same major also meet with the recruit and their family. That is very important, because no coach can really tell a recruit what it is like to be a Nursing, Business, Science, or Education major better than a student-athlete going through the program.

Our coaches and faculty utilize a student management system to communicate daily about attendance, assignments, behavior, and test grades. If there are ever problems, faculty will call or email to communicate with the coach so that everyone can be involved with getting the student-athlete back on the track if they are experiencing difficulties. At the beginning of each year, we meet with all new faculty to discuss our department's expectations for the student-athletes and start the open lines of communication. It is a partnership and commitment to educate the whole person. The actions of everyone are indicative of the value we place on "family." We treat our student-athletes like a member of our family and expect them to treat each other in this same manner.

Today the recruiting cycling is a year-round process. We have a saying in our department that speaks to this. We refer to it as "RDOP"—Recruit Daily or Perish. Every day there is something a coach should be doing to work on their recruiting. Many of our programs are working at least one year ahead. In many cases when a high school freshman or sophomore is identified, the process starts with a handwritten letter or card. That is so important to start relationship-building.

Usually what is communicated in that handwritten letter is where a coach saw the recruit competing and what qualities were demonstrated that caught the coach's attention. This really tells the recruit that something they did made them stand out to that coach. That cannot be accomplished with a typical form letter that many people send. When contact information is easily available like a phone number, a coach will call as soon as they can to communicate that same message. On some occasions, coaches will call while the recruit is competing and leave a voice mail message.

Much of this early identification happens during the summer and at times can happen at camps or ID events coaches are either working or attending. Once that contact has been made, a first call is usually scheduled to gauge interest. Our best recruiters want to be the first to communicate with a student-athlete, because that makes a lasting impression. That phone call is then followed up with one to the mom and dad.

Today that is very important because parents want and expect to be involved in the recruiting process. To not include them is a critical mistake. It is also important because a coach needs to determine which parent will have the most influence on a final decision. Starting that communication early with parents will help in determining where hurdles may come to enroll and retain the student at your institution.

The next step is getting that student-athlete and their family on your campus for a visit. We have a lot of visits during the summer months, especially with out-of-state recruits. So many big recruiting events happen in the Atlanta metro region. Our coaches work with those families while they are in the area and get them to visit during these events. As the summer winds down and we enter the fall semester, many of the local recruits visit campus during.

In most cases, coaches want recruits to complete their applications and have test scores sent before visiting campus. This allows the coaches to gather much of the information they will need while the students are on their visit. The recruit will learn about the academic scholarships they qualify for, and if they have completed FASFA or bring the previous year's tax return, our financial aid officers can give them an idea if they will qualify for any need-based financial aid or for the Pell Grant. These are all critical pieces of information that lead to a final decision. We want a visit to accomplish the goal of providing that information to a family.

Today, especially on the women's side, student-athletes want to make a decision in the fall of the junior year—like their Division I and Division II teammates who have signed scholarships. It is not unusual for many of our women's programs to already have commitments from student-athletes during the fall of their junior year. Working this far ahead has been beneficial for our programs. It requires that our coaches work on a 12-month recruiting cycle.

In most of the male programs we do not see the same things happening. Men will wait to see if a scholarship opportunity will present itself to them. It is so critical to get the young men on campus during the summer and early during the fall semester. Their timetable tends to be a year behind the females. Getting all the information into Admissions and Financial Aid before the visit is still critically important. Families have a limited amount of time that they will dedicate to the recruiting process. When you get a family on campus you must be productive. You need to make a great impression to enroll a student-athlete. That takes a team effort on a visit day. Everyone needs to shine and present a consistent message and answer the important questions the recruit and the family may have.

It is a perceived disadvantage by many that Division III is not able to award athletic scholarships. However, that is one of our greatest advantages. The perspective that we have is that a student-athlete will be awarded their academic scholarship based on what they have earned in the classroom and by how well they have done with their test scores.

This also gives our coaches the opportunity to focus on the fact that our student-athletes are first and foremost "students." Their academics come first. The other advantage we have in Division III is that we can contact a prospect once they become a freshman and we also do not have the recruiting "dead periods" that Division I and II have. We can stay in constant contact with a recruit and their family.

To recruit and retain student-athletes effectively takes a very concentrated effort. You must understand and embrace the philosophy of the institution. We have built a culture to first attract quality coaches that are committed to that culture. We have made decision that retention is the key to having solid healthy rosters that graduate their student-athletes. We have also been committed to excellence in all our pursuits. These things have helped us grow and achieve the goals and high standards we have for our department.

We are fortunate to have incredible leadership from our president and senior staff, and have tremendous collaboration with our Admissions and Financial Aid staff to accomplish these goals. Finally, open lines of communication with our faculty with a focus on the student success has been essential. This has been the formula for success that we have followed.

ESSAY: JULIA M. SCHMITZ AND MELISSA TINGLE—HIGH IMPACT PRACTICES

High-Impact Practices (HIPs) were purposely introduced in the fall of 2017 at Piedmont University as part of the institution's Quality Enhancement Plan (QEP). This plan, based on the research of George Kuh,[10] is aimed at increasing select aspects of student learning at the undergraduate level, specifically: Undergraduate Research & Creative Inquiry, and Global Learning. In addition to these two HIPs, we are focused on developing student leadership as a

HIP. While there was some evidence at the course and programmatic levels that instructors already practiced these HIPs at Piedmont, we wanted to have a more purposeful implementation of these throughout the institutional culture.

As part of the QEP, we reserved some of our budget to fund novel High-Impact Practice ideas from students, faculty, and staff. This allowed students, faculty, and staff to try out novel ideas, participate in a conference to bring back new ideas, or implement a new research project. This also showed the students, faculty, and staff that we were invested in bringing HIPs to our campus. After only three years of offering funding, we funded 50 projects totaling over $46,000. Any student, faculty, or staff that received funding was required to present either through our Center for Teaching and Learning or through a yearly showcase we were developing for students.

Lessons Learned

Finley and McNair reference research by Kuh by stating that "high-impact practices have a pronounced effect on the experiences of underserved students . . . showing positive relationships between high-impact or engaged experiences and different measures of student achievement."[11] To that end we have specifically been looking at our data in various ways. For example, we disaggregate the data by underserved students, which we define as ethnic minority, Pell-eligible, and first-generation.

Until fall of 2017, first-generation data was self-reported on the Admissions application, and rarely did students self-report. Fall of 2018 was the first time we were able to get a clearer picture of the population of first-generation students we have (approximated 30 percent). In 2019, we celebrated our first National First-Generation Day. In 2020, we increased the celebration and surveyed faculty and staff to determine who among them is also first generation. This will allow us to match first gen faculty and staff with students to form a type of mentor relationship. Had we not thought to start collecting this data in 2017 we wouldn't have had a picture of who some of our underserved students were.

One of the major problems with measuring the effect of HIPs is that there isn't a control group. All students have the opportunity to participate in any of the experiences and thus we cannot fully measure the impact of HIPs as compared to a student who didn't have access to any HIPs. We have mitigated this issue by comparing students who participate in various HIPs to those who do not. We even track the number of HIPs a student participates in, as well as which HIPs to see if there are certain HIPs that are more impactful than others.

Undergraduate Research and Creative Inquiry

During the first three years of the five-year quality enhancement plan (QEP), the HIP we developed most fully focused on undergraduate research and creative inquiry. Through this HIP, we wanted to provide intentional opportunities for students to apply problem-based learning to disciplinary and interdisciplinary scholarship. Some departments, like Natural Sciences, already had strong research courses and opportunities in place for upper-level juniors and seniors, but we wanted to increase these research experiences across the entire campus as well as weave them into lower-division classes.

We also wanted to develop a campus-wide symposium event that would offer students the opportunity to exhibit research and creative inquiry projects, as well as give us data to assess the effectiveness of HIP implementation. To do so, we had to focus on areas of funding, awareness, participation (including projects and open houses), and data collection.

Funding. Faculty were encouraged to apply for funds to help support the cost of research, especially if bringing new ideas to a lower-division course or creating a cross-discipline project. One project we funded allowed for a faculty member and a student to attend a conference which highlighted a piece of machinery they had obtained for a fabrication lab in the Art Department. The faculty and student brought what they learned back to campus and have used the machine for several cross-discipline collaborations: student chairs for art shows, face shields for first responders in the local community, and a working model (Enviroscape) that demonstrates how various types of pollution can affect a community for the Environmental Science department.

Raising Symposium Hype. Not only did we increase the funding for research projects, we had to develop ways of getting the campus excited about the institution-wide Symposium event that was implemented in the second year of QEP. We invited a renowned research professor from a different peer institution to generate interest in the research day. The speaker presented to faculty and students in various sessions throughout the time she was on campus, and created multiple small workings groups for research idea creation. We launched the online application for the Symposium day while the speaker was on campus to continue to build on the excitement created with her visit.

Solidifying Participation. To ensure we had a successful first Symposium, the planning committee worked with academic deans and the heads of different co-curricular projects (Summer Travel Study, Alternate Spring Break, and Experiential Learning) to develop participation goals for each of their areas. This not only ensured the planning committee was working tirelessly to encourage students to participate but so were others that had direct knowledge of what their students were doing. This ensured we had a higher percentage of participation and overall buy-in.

We also found that when a faculty or staff member personally reached out to a student to encourage them to present on a project from class, the student was more likely to apply, because they wanted to make the faculty and/or staff member proud. Due to the hard work of the committee, the academic deans, and the heads of the different cocurricular projects, our first Symposium exceeded our goals. Our first Symposium had a goal of 78 presentations, and we had 84 presentations with 132 students presenting. What made this Symposium a success was encouraging faculty to think outside of the box for the presentations.

Types of Projects. For the most part, students submitted traditional presentations and posters on research or class collaboration projects. Through conversations with the faculty advisor for our institution's literary journal, we created a panel that combined the classes working on the writing and art pieces for the journal. This allowed students to have a broader understanding of the hard work that goes into this yearly publication, as well as increased participation from lower-division classes. Our English department selected the top four essays from the first-year writing class. These students read their papers out loud at the Symposium, modeling what they would do at a professional conference in their respective discipline.

Open House. Probably one of the most unique aspects of the day was what we have termed "Open Houses." As mentioned earlier, members of our Art Department had been able to attend a conference on digital fabrication using HIP funding, and then used their own departmental funds to procure the technology. During the Open House, they showcased the Fabrication Lab

(Fab Lab), which houses a laser cutter, CNC (Computer Numeric Control) router, and 3D printers. Students discussed the projects they built, hacked, or created a prototype for.

Another Open House featured our campus wetlands. Students and faculty discussed the research they participated in, as well as showcased some of the macroinvertebrates that are found in the streams leading into the wetlands. Students are researching the beaver community effect on the environment as well as different bacteria found in the soil.

Collecting Data. Data from the event shows that it was huge success and numerous students remarked that they learned a lot from the first year and could not wait to participate in next year's event. Ten months after the event we conducted focus groups with students who presented at the Symposium. We found that 83 percent of the students had an increased interest in research, 100 percent of the students felt their communication skills had strengthened, 77 percent felt this event increased their preparation for career/graduate school, and 61 percent remarked on the interdisciplinary exposure the day provided for them.

When looking at the retention rate from spring semester to fall semester of the students who presented at the Symposium versus those who did not, we saw a greater retention of the students who presented. We attribute this to the experiences the student had that allowed them to present at the Symposium, such as the mentored experience and delving deeper into their discipline. This event has been so successful that more departments are looking at ways to involve lower-level students in mentored research. One department has created a class for sophomores and juniors where they can work alongside a senior performing research or directly with a faculty member on their own project.

Lessons Learned. To ensure we have a successful Symposium each year we rely on faculty and/or staff to personally encourage students to present. Most of the times, the students probably haven't thought about the project they are working on to be eligible to present at the Symposium, so having the faculty member encourage them increases the number of submissions. We also aim to hold an event during the submission process to educate students on what constitutes as research and having ways for the students to submit their projects at the event so they don't have to remember to do it later.

Global Learning

The second HIP we focused on is Global Learning. This HIP is designed to provide intentional opportunities for students to engage in mindful exploration of cross-cultural differences, as well as provide avenues for participating in transformative cultural experiences. We accomplish this through our Alternate Spring Break and Summer Travel Study programs. During Alternate Spring Break, students travel to other cities in the United States and participate in volunteer opportunities such as building houses, while exploring the intersection of academic study and vocational aspiration. Summer travel study involves students traveling abroad while completing course requirements for a general education and an elective course.

Alternate Spring Break. The Alternate Spring Breaks are offered at no cost to the students, but there is a selection process for the trip. Previous trips include travel to New Orleans, Orlando, and Nashville, among other cities. When the students return from the trip, they must submit a written reflection on how the experience enhanced their education at Piedmont. Lastly, the students present as a panel at our annual Symposium to share what they have learned. Our retention rate from the previous three years of trips has been approximately 70 percent of students who participated.

Summer Travel Study. Our summer travel is unique in that the cost of the travel to the different countries is included in the tuition cost for the courses the students take. This does not overburden students with program costs. Countries that our students have visited include France, Switzerland, Ireland, Japan, Peru, and Germany, among other countries.

Funding. During an event to promote summer travel study, students expressed concerns about the financial burden of the trips, even though the cost of the trip was the summer tuition for the two courses the students would take. To help ease this burden, summer travel grants were created from the QEP budget for Pell eligible students only (approximately 40–50 percent of our student population). The students wrote essays about how this trip would enhance their academic experience at Piedmont College.

The essays were blind reviewed and scored based on a rubric that assessed how the summer travel will impact them in a meaningful way, provide a strong connection between the trip and their academic interests and/or courses, and how they will benefit from the experience. All essays had three reviewers and the scores were averaged to rank the essays. Our first year we were only able to fund the tuition costs for six students. In the subsequent years, we increased the number of students (10 in year 2; 14 in year 3). The students who received this funding were required to write thank you notes, providing a short reflection essay upon return, and participated in future events promoting Summer Travel.

Data Collection. While the rubric remained the same across the years, we did update the weight for each category putting more emphasis on how the summer travel will impact them in a meaningful way. When looking at the effect of summer travel on our retention, we had a 75 percent retention rate from the May 2018 trips. We had an 85 percent retention rate from students who participated in our May 2019 trips. Due to COVID-19, we were unable to send students on summer travel trips in May 2020.

Leadership

The last HIP we have focused on has been Leadership. We are aiming to provide intentional opportunities for students to apply their knowledge and skills to real world issues while reflecting on their identity, self-efficacy, citizenship, social responsibility, and knowledge of their field. We track the number of students who participate in leadership roles across the campus, from peer tutors, to mentoring first-year students in our SAIL (Summer Bridge) program, to club and organization leaders, to athletic leaders, and students who participated in our leadership training.

Student leaders or those who have participated in leadership training are asked to fill out a survey in the spring to score their satisfaction with leadership at Piedmont. Based on a 7-point scale, questions are asked such as how valuable the leadership training was, as well as questions specific to the student organization in which they are leaders. Students rated highest in the following categories: share knowledge, ethics/value actions, passion for goal achievement, awareness of others, and leadership training value.

We also performed focus groups with the students. We asked about the skills they gained in their leadership roles, how participation in leadership has prepared them for their next step, and how has the experience outside the classroom impacted the in-classroom experience. From these focus groups, the following themes emerged: importance of communication and collaboration, playing an active role in the organization, the real-world experience they gained, working with faculty, and the importance of classroom engagement.

In tracking the students who are leaders in the various roles we do see high retention rates. Our highest retention rate has been from students who are members of clubs and organization which provides different ways for them to be involved at school outside of the academic experience. We have also seen a high retention of students who participated in leadership training and are seeing a gradual increase each year of our peer tutors.

If More Resources Available

If we had access to more funding, the first thing we would want to do is to develop a more informative website for the Symposium. Currently, our website showcases articles written about our previous research days. We would like to have videos that show how to create a good submission application, how to do meaningful library research and use their resources better, how to create an oral presentation, and how to create a poster presentation.

We would also like to include commonly asked questions on a section of the website so that students, faculty, and staff could understand the process a little better. Lastly, we would like to showcase some of our previous presentations better. This could be by including snippets from an oral presentation or a poster and the accompanying video that summarizes the key points. We could also use a dedicated person to optimize our Symposium website and leading the event.

With more resources we could also increase the number of students who were able to travel in our summer travel study programs. We have been able to provide grants for a small number of students to travel, but there are many others who apply and can't afford to travel without the grant. This experience has a huge impact on the students' learning about other cultures. Students always return from these experiences changed for the better. This experience is usually the first time the students have traveled abroad, so it is a great way to introduce them to another country and most of the logistics are prepared for them, but they still learn how to navigate in a foreign country.

CODA—RETTIG

Besides the tremendous student support, programming, and organizations expounded in the previous essays, there are other transformative opportunities your institution can put into place. These range from curricular options to other student support programs and procedures.

For example, the work of President Jeffrey Docking of Adrian College has been discussed previously in this book. With the Council of Independent Colleges, he began an astonishing new collaborative effort of private colleges and universities across the nation in the Rize consortium. The premise of the consortium is straightforward and fiscally responsible. It allows institutions across the country to pool resources together for shared majors. [Information on the LCMC/Rize consortium can be found at: www.thelcmc.org.].

Starting a new academic major or program is often financially prohibitive for universities. The personnel costs along with other overhead expenses make such efforts difficult. However, working in collaboration with other institutions, such personnel and infrastructure costs are nearly entirely mitigated.

Say your institution has an academic minor with low enrollments. If you could add an additional six courses, you could create a major. However, another pre-approved institution in the consortium already offers these necessary courses and have the instructors to teach them. Your students, via an online learning platform, could take these courses and earn a major from your institution. Your institution does not pay for this, nor do they need to pay for extra professors or associated overhead costs. There is only a modest fee for the students. These students can remain at your college and not need to transfer and could benefit from all the other experiences provided at your institution.

Milestones are another organizational process that universities can put into place to help retain students and keep them on track to graduation. Every college and university have critical junctures along a student's pathway that can "make or break" the student's academic career. Identification of these key milestones or expectations is critical, and most of these areas are already well known.

For example, students who take a full credit load are more likely to remain in college. If they take too few credits, the light at the end of the tunnel is too dim—too far away, and the tendency of students is to lose motivation to continue. So, a milestone or expectation is the number of credits earned per semester. Similarly, maintaining a GPA of 3.0 is important. Should a student fall below this threshold for more than one semester, it can be difficult to earn a grade point expected to graduate.

Students who declare an academic major early in their careers are also more likely to retain and to graduate. While students can certainly change their majors, the focus of choosing a major helps to ensure a student will stay on track. Choosing a major prior to their sophomore year is important. Similarly, early and routine visits to the Career Services offices has proven to be critical to student success. Like choosing an academic major early on is important, it is equally important to identify a career path. Again, the focus of a profession keeps students on track for success.

Other milestones include getting involved in campus organizations or affinity groups. For example, freshmen should be encouraged to become acquainted with different organizations and participate. By the time they are sophomores they can become active members, and later they can become leaders within their organizations. Affinity with academic clubs, athletic teams, theater or musical groups, student newspaper, and the like are such transformational experiences that make students want to return the next year; they can offer the hook that students need for success.

NOTES

1. Jeffrey Docking. *Crisis in Higher Education: A Plan to Save Small Liberal Arts Colleges in America* (East Lansing, MI: Michigan State University Press, 2015).
   Karen Doss Bowman. "Shifting Demographics." *Trusteeship:* Association of Governing Boards of Universities and Colleges (March/April, 2020), *28*(2): 20–25.
2. Ibid. Docking.
3. Bowman. "Shifting Demographics."
4. Jeffrey Selingo. "The New Generation of Students: How Colleges Can Recruit, Teach, and Serve Gen Z." Washington, DC: *The Chronicle of Higher Education*, 2018.
5. Dana Schwieger and Christine Ladwig. "Reaching and Retaining the Next Generation: Adapting to the Expectations of Gen Z in the Classroom." *Information Systems Education Journal* (June 2018), *16*(3): 50–52.
6. Terrel Rhodes. "The Changing Nature of Work and Careers," Washington, DC: Association of American Colleges & Universities, *Liberal Education* (Summer/Fall 2019), *105*(3/4): 8.

Rhodes goes on to share five fundamental aspects of necessary academic change:

- Transitioning from a system of credits tied to seat time to one of demonstrating competency and proficiency
- Moving from an emphasis on majors and general education to a focus on the learner's entire educational pathway
- Shifting from traditional letter grades to the application of learning demonstrated in students' work over time
- Foregoing learning approaches based on knowledge transmission in favor of approaches focusing on meaning- and sense-making
- Instead of providing access to engaged learning for the favored few, ensuring high impact practices (HIPs) are available to all students, everywhere. (8)

He concludes that ePortfolios and comprehensive student records (CSRs) are tools to measure and capture these practices. (10)

7. George Kuh. *High-Impact Practices: What They Are, Who Has Access to Them, and Why they Matter* (Washington, DC: Association of American Colleges and Universities, 2008).

8. Laura Hamilton, Josipa Roksa, and Kelly Nielsen., "Providing a 'Leg Up': Parental Involvement and Opportunity Hoarding in College." SAGE: *American Sociological Association* (2018), *91*(2): 118. Journals.sagepub.com/home/soe.

9. Tom Rath. *Discover Your CliftonStrengths* (New York, NY: Gallup Press, 2007), 12.

10. Kuh, George. *High-Impact Practices: What They Are, Who Has Access to Them, and Why They Matter* (Washington, DC: Association of American Colleges and Universities, 2008).

11. Finley, Ashley, and McNair, Tia. Assessing Underserved Students' Engagement in High-Impact Practices. 2013. Retrieved from https://www.aacu.org/sites/default/files/files/assessinghips/AssessingHIPS_TGGrantReport.pdf.

Chapter 5

Strategic Enrollment Management and Planning

The SEM and SEP

The previous chapters expressed numerous strategies to increase student enrollments, retention, and ultimately student success. Strategies and initiatives range from the curricular to the cocurricular, from recruiting and marketing to the use of new technologies and student support systems. All of these require an integrative and collaborative approach with a unitary vision of student success. In order to make these approaches work in an effective and efficient manner, a robust strategic enrollment management planning process must be implemented.

The first necessary step will be the selection of an enrollment management leader—most often a Vice President for Enrollment Management. The multifold role of the Enrollment Management leader is to communicate, educate, coordinate, and plan. This helps to build a campus culture of enrollment planning, as well as the contributions necessary for every faculty and staff member in recruiting and retaining students.

This leader should establish an enrollment management team for the purpose "to educate a broad range of stakeholders and engage them in the important role of influencing enrollment on your campus."[1] Pope and Davies further elaborate on this point by explaining that this breaks down institutional silos and creates collaborations for student success.

Strategic Enrollment Planning (SEP) is a relatively newer phenomenon compared to the broader based strategic planning efforts well known to industry, nonprofit organizations, and institutions of higher learning. In fact, SEP should flow from, and be an integral part of, broader university strategic planning. There is both a science and an art to all such planning endeavors—to creating change. "Enterprise change management . . . involves embedding change management in an institution's roles, structures, processes, projects, and leadership competencies."[2]

In AGB's *Trusteeship*, Larry Shinn has provided an erudite analysis of enrollment management.[3] He listed six questions trustees, senior leaders, and faculty leaders together need to consider:

1. Have we studied the impact of the precipitous enrollment decline in 2026 on our college's admissions territories and adjusted our enrollment/revenue projections accordingly?
2. Have we performed an inclusive "financial stress test" for our institutions that includes data from both internal (e.g., net tuition/income trends, discount rate, etc.) and external (e.g., endowment market projections, Moody's rating, etc.) sources?
3. Do our current academic structures, curricula, and learning goals provide our students not only depth in their liberal arts or professional majors but also holistic, multidisciplinary, integrative problem-solving skills that we assess?
4. What is the best way for us to organize our teaching/learning resources (i.e., curricular, faculty, student support, etc.) to enhance student learning in a financially sustainable way?
5. Is our current strategic plan strategic and, if not, how best can our institution's leadership create a strategic planning process that will address in innovative ways current external challenges to our institution's sustainability?
6. What issues in our institution's shared governance and decision-making culture do we need to address to enable real innovation in our strategic thinking and planning?

Indeed, without financial considerations, all strategic thinking efforts will be fraught with peril. The accounting and structural elements, whether they are versions of Revenue Centered Management (RCM) or Open Source Alternative Budgeting or other, are less important than the process. "The way forward is therefore not to double down on competition. The way forward is to cooperate across divisions. And we can't do that without making budgeting more transparent and collaborative."[4]

In their review of the literature, Smith and colleagues expressed: "To become nimble, institutions should focus on two areas:

1) 'Creation of the environment where nimbleness can flourish reflected in the organization's leadership, culture, and approach to change roles; and
2) Creation of the application structures and processes that drive successful execution reflected in the organization's portfolio of initiatives and implementation architecture.'"[5]

In an interview conducted by Karen Doss Bowman, Youngstown State University Board of Trustees member Molly Seals spoke of the need for inclusive leadership involvement in planning:

Preparing for the demographic storm is not just about attracting and retaining a broader base of students . . . [i]t's also about "creating an infrastructure of systems and actions that will allow us to be a more versatile and flexible organization that can react and adapt nimbly to such a rapid decline in the population of high school graduates."[6]

It should go without saying, but it must be said nevertheless, strategic enrollment thinking must be purposefully collaborative and inclusive with all parties. Planning without the university leadership integrally involved will flounder and devolve into chaos. Planning without those responsible for carrying out the strategies will not be embraced nor will be realistic and therefore will collapse under its own weight.

The two final essays of this book address the sundry issues related to strategic enrollment planning. First, Dr. P.J. Woolston brings decades of experience and wisdom to strategic enrollment management and subsequent planning efforts. He has served as a senior leader at different public and private universities and will provide the philosophy and an expansive 30,000-foot view of such planning. He will conclude with descriptive details with regard to how to carry out actual planning—the science of SEP.

Dr. Perry Rettig has held multiple senior leadership roles on both the academic, and enrollment and student affairs divisions in both public and private institutions. This broad portfolio provides him a unique perspective in both broad-based strategic planning and strategic enrollment planning. His essay expresses actual past and ongoing SEP efforts he has led at Piedmont

University—the art of SEP. Piedmont's strategies and initiatives in SEP 1.0 have already shown success. They are now poised to begin SEP 2.0.

ESSAY: P. J. WOOLSTON—THE SCIENCE OF STRATEGIC ENROLLMENT PLANNING

Strategic planning can be a difficult commitment to make. The scope and magnitude of the work is significant, requiring great perseverance from all involved. This is not just a commitment of time and resources, but a commitment to collaboration and transparency which is sometimes a bigger commitment to make. In many cases the returns are not immediate. On the other hand, failing to think strategically and long-term about institutional enrollment can and often does result in an uncomfortable stasis. At some point the student experience will suffer and enrollment will plateau or decline as the institution is overtaken by competitor institutions that have been more strategic in their efforts.

By its very nature strategic enrollment planning takes significant time and preparation, both to execute and to realize the benefits. Some returns will be immediate, but the most important aspects and results will only yield returns with consistent commitment, execution, and accountability. For this reason, strategic enrollment planning is obviously important, but often not perceived as urgent. Therefore, the strategic planning process requires institutional dedication and fortitude.

The purpose of strategic enrollment planning is to anchor the institution within the environmental realities surrounding it. It "connects mission, current state, and changing environments to long-term enrollment and fiscal health, resulting in a concrete, written plan of action." The plan itself serves as a direct link between the institutional strategic plan and the actual recruitment plans for each student population.

On the other hand, strategic enrollment planning is not the set of actual student recruitment plans. It has greater long-term implications and requires greater commitment and investment, resulting in more impactful returns. A strategic enrollment plan covers several years, and necessarily outlives annual recruitment plans. Those plans, while also important, serve a distinctly different role.

Consequently, it can be easy to under-budget for strategic enrollment planning. One of the most important steps in initiating the process is planning adequate funding. Both the process itself and the execution of the plan will need to be adequately funded both in terms of fiscal commitment and (even more importantly and more expensively) time commitment. To be successful, planning should include the entire university.

Everyone involved will need to have enough capacity, discipline, and time (or release time) for the process. The cost of time through salaries and wages already constitutes the greatest expenses of any college or university, and our payrolls rarely boast excess or even additional capacity. If allowance is not made for those who will be involved, particularly for those playing leadership roles, the likelihood of success for the process will decline.

The other cost (financial) is also significant and often underrated. Institutions may be able to avoid a fiscal cost up front by managing the process internally rather than hiring a consultant or a firm to do so, however an important end result of the process will be a series of initiatives specifically designed to grow or improve enrollment within the context of that institution's needs. If these initiatives are inadequately funded (or worse, unfunded entirely), the recommendations of the process and the plan will essentially be moot.

As mentioned previously, there are two primary ways to approach the execution of strategic enrollment planning: either hiring a consultant or a firm to guide the institution over the course of the process, or managing the process internally with existing staff. There are advantages and disadvantages for each of these. Many schools elect to hire a consultant because of the expertise and experience, the credibility, and the objective and external view such a professional can bring.

There is a reason this approach is so popular; in some ways it is actually easier because it can take less institutional discipline and it is usually more efficient. The school is engaging an accountability partner who can not only lead the team through a formally defined process but can also follow up to make sure each person fulfills their responsibility at each step. This partner has usually guided several other institutions through a similar process and so already knows the most effective techniques as well as pitfalls to avoid. They bring significant resources to bear beyond their expertise in the form of materials and support staff.

On the other hand, this approach is expensive. There are financial implications because of the fees associated with such an engagement, but there are time implications as well. Whichever professional is serving as the institutional lead for strategic enrollment planning (usually a Vice President for Enrollment Management or similarly designated professional) will need to devote significant time to interaction with and management of the outside agency.

That person will also serve as the chief point person back to all of the institutional partners involved in the process. There are multiple options for hiring a partner, ranging from short-term consultations to sweeping long-term engagements. Many partners provide an initial assessment and diagnosis which often yields valuable, actionable insights.

The primary alternative to hiring a partner is to manage the process entirely in-house. This approach allows for maximum flexibility and control, but that same advantage is the most problematic aspect. It is the nature of complex organizations to manage multiple simultaneous enterprises, and therefore the person responsible for leading this process inevitably has multiple responsibilities and commitments in other areas as well.

Oftentimes this person has limited experience running strategic enrollment planning and may be caught off guard by unanticipated roadblocks throughout the process. This approach is generally less efficient because the leader is often essentially inventing the wheel as they go along. It is imperative that an institution taking this approach take advantage of the various and plentiful resources treating strategic enrollment planning.

There are numerous texts from external organizations in both the private and not-for-profit sectors (e.g., Ruffalo Noel-Levitz, AACRAO, etc.), as well as various courses, forums, and other learning opportunities. An institution should also not neglect the willing collaboration of multiple people throughout the higher education community: direct colleagues who have executed the process before, potential partners willing to engage in partnerships of limited scope, and actual collateral from successful processes elsewhere. For instance, many public universities are required by law to publish their strategic enrollment plans and studying these documents can provide extraordinary insight and guidance.

Most professionals in higher education share the common mission of fostering student success and are therefore more than willing to help, especially where actual competition or conflict of interest is low. Anyone electing to approach strategic enrollment planning in this way should make every effort to maximize the use of reliable external resources.

Organization is of the utmost importance for a successful planning process, and timing is everything. There is actually more value in the planning process than in the actual plan itself (the end result) because of the way it draws together people from the entire university into a common cause. Because of that need for inclusion, transparency and communication are absolutely critical, as is the ability to manage expectations (i.e., with senior leadership, faculty, staff involvement, etc.). It is therefore important that the strategic enrollment planning process be mapped as closely as possible to the academic calendar because then it will be most in sync with the rhythm of all involved.

There are three distinct phases to the process: data collection and analysis, strategy development, and the actual writing of the plan. The first phase of data collection and analysis lends itself most naturally to the fall semester. Once classes have resumed, people usually have enough relief in their capacity to turn their attention to this initial phase.

This includes working closely with data by establishing key enrollment indicators (KEIs, or the metrics that will indicate how the plan is proceeding toward success), and planning for how to monitor those data (the establishment of dashboards, shared drives, regular and consistent reporting, etc.). This also includes an environmental scan to determine honestly and objectively the market position of the institution (reputation, selectivity, competition, etc.) and a clear understanding of the external influences on the institution (such as demographic and industry projections).

The second phase of the planning process focuses on strategy development. A comprehensive strategy development plan includes casting a wide initial net, or essentially brainstorming. This is not about generating as many ideas as possible, rather it creates a greater sense of inclusion by involving all the disparate parties of the campus (when done right) and generates not more but better (often parallel) ideas that can be developed and pursued.

Once a relatively comprehensive list has been generated, some subset of that list should be identified as likely options for implementation and eventual success based on an evaluation of each idea for its feasibility, cost, and potential ROI (return on investment). This shorter list should then be assigned, initiative by initiative, to various members of the group managing the process as reflected by expertise and in order to share the load of developing so many plans.

Once these plans have been developed they can be compared and prioritized on a more level playing field, after which a final subset (usually at least four and very rarely more than eight) can be selected for actual implementation. That implementation will then need to be very thoroughly mapped out including identification of the parties responsible, major milestones, steps between those milestones, and most importantly metrics of accountability that indicate what the ultimate goals are and what the institution should experience along the way verifying that the idea is sound and is in fact being implemented successfully.

When the process is executed thoughtfully and well, the final step of the process, actually writing the plan, is usually the simplest part because the work has already been done! The plan itself should be as concise and readable as possible. It should include a one-page executive summary because many invested partners (for instance, senior leadership, trustees, etc.) will want to glean quickly and efficiently the most salient insights relevant to their own unique perspective.

The plan should include context for the strategic enrollment planning process, detail about the process that has been executed over the course of the year, who was involved, what data and information they explored, and of course, a detailed summary of the strategic initiatives adopted as well as their plans for realization. The plan also should include data, key enrollment indicators, and other historical reference points as appendices, and especially enrollment history and projections.

These numbers in particular will indicate important factors for all student populations such as new student enrollment quantities, retention rates, graduates or degrees awarded, etc. Ideally a big-picture summary of these numbers should be included in the executive summary. A footer for the entire report can indicate at a glance when the plan was written and when it was most recently revised, additional important context.

The plan does not need to be long. Length will be affected by things like institution size, scope, levels of external compliance, and so forth; however, the most usable and readable plans are shorter. Additionally, depending on how the strategic enrollment planning process was conducted, the actual writing of the plan does not have to be significant work. If the leader of the planning process provides a detailed recapitulation to the strategic enrollment management committee after each meeting and significant milestones, the plan can essentially be amalgamated into a single narrative with appropriate commentary of these summaries.

As alluded to here, the core group working through the strategic enrollment management process at the direction of a chief enrollment management officer should be an enrollment management committee or council of some kind. Developing a council that draws comprehensively from across the university is critical to establishing the credibility of the process and the viability of the final plan. There should of course be an administrative core. The most likely partners are key staff from leadership in Admissions and Financial Aid, but also professionals in Student Affairs, Finance, and Institutional Research.

Perhaps the most critical constituency to involve, however, is the faculty. The faculty serve as the single common link to every student experience regardless of student type, program, or history. Faculty should be drawn representatively from across disciplines, degree types, and student populations, in close collaboration with the Provost or Chief Academic Officer.

As with any endeavor, there will need to have careful forethought with respect to faculty load and capacity so as to allow the faculty the ability to contribute meaningfully. Neglecting adequately to involve the faculty, more than any other single factor, will undermine the strategic enrollment planning process and the end result. On the other hand, involving the faculty thoroughly, early and often, will do more to ensure the broad buy-in of the plan than anything.

Simply having a strategic enrollment management council is insufficient unless the members of the group are empowered to represent the planning process to others within the campus community. It is important for the leader of the planning process to give committee members a script. The easiest way to do this is to provide a detailed summary of each committee meeting including assignments made and dates for execution. Then the committee members will be able to recall that summary on demand or as opportunity presents itself with ease from a cellphone if not from memory.

Summarizing immediately and often also compels the leader of the process to be relatively succinct and helps focus participation in subsequent meetings. These summaries will then serve as the first draft outline for the actual plan itself as noted. The frequency for these committee meetings will vary based on the institution, but in general should be approximately three weeks apart. This allows for time in between meetings to gather and analyze data, and to complete other assignments as they come up, and gives the members of the committee relatively new and recent information to share with predictable regularity.

Part of transparency is getting the word out to the entire institution about the enrollment planning process underway, and every opportunity should be taken to publicize what is going on. Aside from enlisting the help of the committee members, there should be a secondary group of key people included on all committee emails.

This group should include senior leadership such as deans, vice presidents, directors, and so on—professionals who are not engaged directly with the work of the committee but who would benefit from knowing what is happening and who will also be able to share progress. Doing this can be as simple as creating separate "CC" distribution list and copying this group on any pertinent communications.

The process leader in particular (as well as anyone else who finds themselves frequently sharing progress) should have several things always at the ready for the entire duration of the project. These include a two-sentence update on the planning process that can be delivered at a moment's notice (the "elevator pitch"), any relevant documentation outlining the process (such as a planning document), the meeting schedule, and a list of the membership of the committee.

This last point is particularly important because one of the most frequent questions that will come up is about who is on the committee. This speaks to the inherent interest that everyone at the school will have to ensure that the population of students that they serve will be adequately represented. Being able immediately to assure anyone that this is the case will alleviate most concerns.

Other opportunities for updates on the process include administrative council meetings, Board of Trustees meetings, open forums, and even creative opportunities to educate the campus about strategic enrollment planning and why it is relevant to the operation now. The process leader should constantly be seeking opportunities to provide updates and should request that opportunity at virtually every appearance the person makes.

Over the course of the process, if done right, the process leader will become known for strategic enrollment planning, having created an identity specifically to it. This person will almost be a "broken record" in championing the process. The goal is that no one on campus is ever surprised about what is going on, let alone that a strategic enrollment plan is being developed. Everyone needs to have the opportunity to weigh in, and their contribution can be evaluated as is appropriate.

The process leader also should be prepared for the inevitable moments when the process does not go exactly according to plan. There will without doubt be times when the gap between what is ideal and what is actually happening will be wider than desired. Faculty and staff will be stretched too thinly and may not be able to contribute as much as they or the leader want or are counting on. Often the people the institution would like to be involved with the process include the same people that are contributing to so many other important campus activities.

Meetings will have to be canceled for one reason or another, and with a tight turnaround for agendas and a limited window to develop and begin implementing the plan, the timeframe will have to be adjusted rather than delayed. It will also certainly be the case that strategy ideation, or brainstorming, will not go exactly as expected. There will be new and original ideas as well as resurrected ones.

There will be excellent ideas with immediate potential and poor ideas fraught with risk. It is absolutely essential that during this process in particular, where emotions run high whether because of passion or vulnerability, the process leader maintain the utmost transparency and collaboration. The leader should trust in the collective wisdom of the group ultimately to select, develop, and fund those initiatives which have the greatest potential for positive impact on student experience and enrollment.

Remember that the most important part of this process is the actual process, not the document itself. The document is educational in nature and serves as an important artifact of culture, but the process will change the institution for the better in the immediate term just for executing it with rigor, and in the long term through faithful adherence to the adopted initiatives. The plan itself is also a living document, not solely an index.

There are two particularly effective ways to ensure that the strategic enrollment plan remains viable. First, the strategic enrollment management committee should continue to meet, albeit with less frequency, to review progress to goals and make any necessary adjustments. Second, the plan needs to be updated annually. Some of those revisions will be simpler and lighter and can include fewer people. This will be appropriate when the strategic initiatives will continue largely as planned and are making appropriate progress to goal.

Some of those revisions will be more comprehensive to the point where they are almost a replication of the process. Often the term for a strategic enrollment plan is five years, at which point the plan should be retired and celebrated, and the process should be renewed.

For institutions looking to improve their chances of a successful strategic enrollment planning process, even a modest investment can provide a huge payoff. With only a little bit of funding and an allowance for extra time and capacity, the designated process leader can self-educate on strategic enrollment planning by acquiring and studying enrollment texts, participating in conferences and forums, and networking with colleagues who have executed the process at other institutions.

This kind of thoughtful preparation will enhance the process and therefore the results regardless of whether the institution has chosen to partner with an outside agency or to manage everything internally, and these efforts can be undertaken either prior to beginning the process or simultaneously while managing it. This is a form of professional development from which the college or university will benefit immediately and will enhance significantly both the process and the end plan immeasurably.

Strategic enrollment planning[7] is one of the smartest investments an institution can make. There is literally no disincentive to undertake the process. The individuals involved become better professionals and are able to contribute more fully to institutional success. The campus draws closer through pervasive collaboration. Trust increases throughout the organization, both laterally and horizontally, through transparency and the work to a common goal. Most importantly, the school ensures a brighter future by actually envisioning it and beginning to take concrete, measurable steps to realize that future.

ESSAY: PERRY RETTIG—THE ART OF STRATEGIC ENROLLMENT PLANNING

In 2013 when he was first hired, Perry Rettig served as the Vice President of Academic Affairs at Piedmont College and oversaw all areas under the academic umbrella but was also informally responsible for oversight of enrollment management and student affairs. After several years, the president of the college, with an ambitious goal to significantly increase enrollments, undergraduate retention rates, and residential student populations, created a new position of Vice President for Enrollment Management and Student Affairs (VPEM). Subsequently, Piedmont College has become Piedmont University.

It was noted in the introduction to this chapter that the first necessary step to enrollment management is the selection of an enrollment management leader—most often a Vice President for Enrollment Management. The role of the Enrollment Management leader is to communicate, educate, coordinate, and plan. This helps to build a campus culture of enrollment planning, as well as the contributions necessary for every faculty and staff member in recruiting and retaining students.

In turn, the VPEM will then need to build an enrollment management team to advise and carry out the responsibilities described in the preceding paragraph. At Piedmont University, the formal enrollment management team includes: the Associate Vice President of Undergraduate Admissions, Associate Vice President for Graduate Admissions, Associate Vice President for Student Success, Dean of Students, the Director of Institutional Research, the Registrar, the Director of Financial Aid, the Diversity Coordinator, the VPEM Administrative Assistant, and faculty representatives from each of the colleges, representatives from the Department of Athletics, and representatives from the Business Office.

Routine communication with the executive leadership cabinet is critical. Each Friday afternoon, the Vice President for Enrollment Management and Student Affairs provides an executive admissions summary to his cabinet colleagues. This summary includes an Excel spreadsheet provided by the Office of Undergraduate Admissions which focuses on aggregate data for applications, admits, and deposits for freshmen and transfer students, in separate columns. It also includes discount rates, as well as net and total tuition revenue targets.

The report also disaggregates the same data between the main and the sister campus. In addition, information is shared point-in-time, or year-over-year compared to the last four years. This is essential, for we may show a number of 25 deposits this past week—that doesn't tell anyone anything unless we can put it into context. Is 25 good, expected, or low? So, we compare that to the same date previous years.

Additional information is provided on this Excel spreadsheet. For example, housing deposits are included, again with point-in-time comparisons. Furthermore, high school/transfer student academic profiles are included which indicates the students' previous Grade Point Average (GPA), and norm-referenced test scores such as SAT/ACT. This further captures the student academic tiers from a high of 1 to a low of 5 indicating their composite academic profile score.

A brief narrative is provided along with the Excel spreadsheet. The narrative provides the context to the raw numbers. For example, it will describe the increases compared to the previous week's report. It will express events that happened (e.g., Preview Day or Scholarship Evening) the previous week and what type of events will occur the following week. Similarly, it will provide context compared to the previous years' point-in-time reports. Finally, the narrative will provide a brief analysis of strengths, concerns, and mitigation strategies moving forward.

This narrative will also include similar descriptions for new graduate enrollments, as well as housing deposits. Of further note, from time-to-time a note is provided describing retention data/trends, and data on the number of students who will be graduating at both the undergraduate and graduate levels. This combined data, retention numbers and graduating students, is critical so the university can determine how many students it will need to replace in terms of budgeting and revenue growth. Finally, a narrative is provided on residence halls capacity along with trends—never should senior leadership be caught surprised.

Such routine and regular communication with the President's Cabinet is essential for planning purposes, as well as making strategic initiative adjustments in a timely manner. While less frequent, similar aggregate data, information, and insights are provided to all faculty and staff throughout the year. Opening Day sessions as well as community forum meetings provide these opportunities. Regular written and verbal communications are also provided to academic deans and to the faculty senate who in turn share with their constituents.

The Board of Trustees meets once each fall and spring semesters. The Vice President for Enrollment Management and Student Affairs presents to the Trustee committee responsible for oversight of enrollment management and student life. The VPEM does not make a solo presentation, however; he uses a collaborative team approach. Members of this team presentation include: the Associate Vice President for Undergraduate Admissions, the Associate Vice President for Graduate Admissions, the Director of Financial Aid, the Athletic Director, the Dean of Students, the Associate Vice President of Student Success, the Diversity Coordinator, and the Administrative Assistant to the VPEM. The Registrar joins at times, as well. Two different students join to make this team presentation each semester.

Each session begins with the two students speaking of their experiences at the university and their plans, whether they be graduate school or the workforce, after college. This is followed by an energized interactive session with the board members and the students. Without fail, the trustees always are impressed with the students and find this interaction the highlight of their day.

A PowerPoint presentation is then shared by the VPEM and his direct reports noted above. This is an opportunity for the professional staff to educate the board members about the enrollment context in which we find ourselves, trends, and pertinent data, information and analysis. During the fall meetings, we present insights from this data and information which then informs our goal-setting and subsequent initiatives for the academic year. In other words, we establish the context and then describe our strategic aims for the months ahead. There is ample time provided throughout the meeting for meaningful interaction of board members and professional staff.

The spring semester follows precisely the same format. However, this meeting has a couple of important differences. First, each division leader shares changes in context that have impacted their year. For example, this past year found a good amount of time discussing the impact of the COVID-19 pandemic. Second, rather than describing the goals as we did in the fall, we spend our time reporting the degree to which we succeeded in reaching our goals. Prior to both fall and spring meetings, written reports from each VPEM cabinet member and subunit members are provided to all Board of Trustees officers.

The responsibilities of educating and communicating are ongoing expectations of the leader of Enrollment Management. No surprises should ever catch Board of Trustees members, senior leaders, faculty or staff members off guard. Changes to the environment will occur, new challenges will emerge, and progress will be made, while other plans may need to be jettisoned. However, it is clear that student recruitment, retention, and success are not the sole responsibility of one individual; it is a mutual responsibility which must be shared both horizontally and vertically across the institution. It is the responsibility of the enrollment management leader to coordinate these endeavors.

Just as the VPEM's communication efforts must have both horizontal and vertical features, so too must the coordination efforts be both horizontal and vertical. Both the Enrollment Management Steering Committee and the Retention Vortex include senior leadership, faculty representatives, and unit heads and support staff. Such representation includes members from both campuses, as well as undergraduate and graduate levels. In turn, not only do these cross-divisional members bring unique perspectives to these teams, they are also able to correspond with their own constituent groups in deliberative two-way communication.

To this point we have discussed the educating, communicating, and coordinating duties of the VPEM. The fourth leg of this stool is that of strategic planning. There is a unique approach to strategic enrollment planning apart from the traditional strategic planning. In the previous essay, Dr. Woolston elucidated the sui generis aspects particular to SEP. For this reason, strategic enrollment planning should stand alone, but it also ultimately must be assumed under the broader umbrella of the institutional strategic planning efforts.

Late in 2016, Piedmont College began in earnest its first-ever institution-wide strategic planning efforts. Just prior, it had concluded re-envisioning its mission statement and core values. The services of an external agency were secured to first prepare an ad hoc leadership team, or steering committee, for the framing of the new planning efforts. The next step was to involve various campus constituencies in both a community forum, as well as distinctive groups of trustees, faculty, and staff. Ultimately, after various iterations of the plan were considered by the ad hoc leadership team, a final product was presented to the board of trustees and subsequently approved. It should be noted that enrollment planning was not part of this broader plan.

At this point, initiative leaders and cabinet sponsors were identified. They received additional training, gathered committees, and created objectives, timelines, and metrics for their goals. In this two-year period the Vice President of Advancement and Marketing, and the Vice President of Administration and Finance both resigned. The Vice President for Academic Affairs shifted responsibilities to serve as the first Vice President of Enrollment

Management and Student Affairs. He also assumed the role of oversight of the sister campus.

A new VPAA was hired and interim vice presidents were secured for the other two positions. While such a significant change in senior leadership made the first couple of years of planning and implementation difficult, the work continued and found success. Once a new leadership team was in place, the VPEM secured the services of a pair of outside consultants from Ruffalo Noel-Levitz to help lead strategic enrollment planning efforts over the following three years.

Both consultants served as vice presidents of enrollment management at other institutions, as well as holding consulting responsibilities with a national enrollment planning firm. While they held similar job titles and responsibilities, the nature of their consulting work for Piedmont College was very different.

One consultant focused exclusively on the offices of Financial Aid, Undergraduate Admissions, and Marketing. More particularly, he focused on workflow, communication messaging, policies and protocols, and strategies to increase prospect awareness and applications. The results of his work were immediate and positive. The previous essays of David McMillion and Cindy Peterson highlight these successes.

The work of the second consultant was very different and saw very little overlap. Dr. Woolston served as this consultant, and his essay above elucidated these efforts, in particular. It was the responsibility of the VPEM to coordinate and lead subsequent planning efforts over the next two years working alongside Dr. Woolston.

Dr. Woolston and the college VPEM began with a couple of phone calls and document sharing in preparation for his forthcoming regularly scheduled visits to the campus. Four phases would encompass his visits over the next 18 months: (1) Preparation and Data Collection; (2) Strategy Development; (3) Plan Drafting and Goal Setting; and (4) Implementation. Woolston's first visit served the purpose of educating the SEP steering committee about the planning process. The VPEM created the Steering Committee and prepared them for the visit and helped secure data and documents in preparation for the first visit.

The Steering Committee consisted of the VPEM, the new VPAA, the leaders of Undergraduate and Graduate Admissions, Financial Aid, Marketing,

Student Engagement, Business Office, Athletics, Information Technology, and faculty members from each of the four schools. During Woolston's first visit, it was determined that four action committees needed to be formed: Academic Planning, New Student Enrollment, Athens Campus, and Retention. Steering Committee members would chair each subcommittee, and membership would include other faculty and staff members.

In subsequent campus visits, Woolston and the Steering Committee led these action committees in identification of key performance indicators (KPIs) and more tangible performance indicators. The action committees further spent a great deal of time collecting and analyzing internal data, as well as contextual data of the region, and doing trend analysis. Much of this work was carried out between campus visits. A SWOT analysis was the final piece of the early planning efforts.

These efforts led to initiative ideation where the action committees, under the direction of the Steering Committee, began the process of identifying specific goals and strategies. The original list was purposefully extensive. Woolston then led the committees through an exhaustive process of winnowing down the initiatives to several which would most likely be manageable and successful. This put a great deal of responsibility and work on the shoulders of the action committee chairs. Between campus visits, the chairs led their teams through a series of meetings, and they continued phone call conversations and email exchanges with Woolston.

The process of determining final initiatives was iterative and is discussed by Woolston in the previous essay of this chapter. Using an algorithm for determining new student enrollments and student retention over the next five years, as well as expenses in terms of personnel and other associated costs, the formula could present a return on investment for each initiative. This helped the Steering Committee decide on its final recommendations to be presented to the President's Cabinet for approval. Four final initiatives were chosen:

1. Marketing/Branding/Website Development;
2. Office of Diversity—Diversity Coordinator;
3. Academic Success Advisors—as part of an expanded First Year Experience; and,
4. Transfer Student Admissions Officers (2—1 per each campus).

The first initiative, Marketing/Branding/Website Development, was considered by the Steering Committee as critical to all the other initiatives and was immediately agreed upon in unanimous fashion. It also fit in precisely with the overall institutional strategic plan. The second initiative, an Office of Diversity—Diversity Coordinator, received immediate support, as well. The primary focus of this office/officer would be to support students, specifically underrepresented populations. Therefore, primary emphasis would focus on retention efforts, although recruitment would likely see an impact, too.

The Academic Success Advisors initiative also tied directly to the overall institutional strategic plan. Three new professional student success advisors were hired to help connect students to High Impact Practices (HIPs), to affinity groups, to get involved in experiential learning opportunities, and to career services opportunities. This initiative primarily focused on retention efforts but would likely show a modest impact on recruitment. These three new hires would be considered Phase I of this initiative to create a new and more robust First Year Experience (FYE) program.

The final initiative was to hire two Transfer Student Admissions Officers (1 per each campus). With the largely untapped adult student population, a new focus with dedicated staff needed to be addressed. Further, both Demorest and Athens campuses have unique demographic challenges. This initiative clearly addressed recruitment goals, but these hires have yet to be realized.

A number of other initiatives were considered so necessary and/or inexpensive to implement that they were approved by the Steering Committee and Senior Administration to be enacted immediately during this planning process. These included: creating new 3rd spaces and upgrades to student technology; starting a new Admitted Student Day in the spring; and adding several new academic programs. The programs included an MA in Psychology, MS in Speech Pathology, Coaching Endorsement in Education, and a Business Endorsement in Hospitality Management.

Further low-hanging fruit included the purchase/implementation of an enterprise student success software system, and the hiring of an additional counselor along with the purchase of a mental health app for students. These latter initiatives created the need for a new organizational structure, which was approved, for the division of Student Affairs. The new structure of Student Affairs has two branches: Student Life and Student Success.

The university has begun to move from planning (SEP) to management (SEM). It is now in a process of continual data collection, analysis, evaluation, and recalibration. From these original efforts and analysis, the university will move into SEP 2.0. Much of the original SEP focused on the "low hanging fruit," and many initiatives therefore were basic necessities in the campus enrollment planning efforts. SEP 2.0 will aim for more significant initiatives aligning with an overall transformational vision and strategic plan for the entire institution.

The SEP Steering Committee has already begun to discuss planning efforts of SEP 2.0. Such efforts will likely focus more on: new academic programs and delivery methods, academic program recruitment/retention targets, graduate enrollments, student retention, and alignment with broader university planning initiatives.

CODA—PERRY RETTIG

Indeed, the role of the Vice President for Enrollment Management is critical to the survival and growth of the institution. Through the recruitment and retention efforts of this office, tuition and auxiliary revenues are responsible for over 90 percent of the university's operating budget. Educating, communicating, coordinating, and planning are the central duties of this senior leader, and these endeavors reach every part of the institution. The work is complex, ever-changing and dynamic, and not for the faint-hearted. Yet, the vocation may be the most rewarding leadership position on any college campus.

Enrollment Management can only be considered successful when our students show success. Student success can easily be measured with metrics of retention and graduation rates. But, most critically, other measurements must be considered: job placement rates, graduate school placement rates, alumni giving/engagement, community participation, and satisfaction both during and post college.

Rutter cites eight strategies colleges must administer in order to improve student success[8]:

1. Enhanced onboarding: introduce them to their advisor; offer summer bridge program

2. A robust first-year experience: study and time management skills, major exploration
3. Data-informed proactive advising: early alerts; courses with high DFW rates
4. Early exposure to career planning: career choices matching and alumni connections
5. Expanded access to experiential learning activities: internships; hands-on learning
6. Enhanced student support services: special financial aid, childcare, etc.
7. Fostering a success-oriented mindset and sense of belonging: engage in affinity group
8. Removing institutional obstacles to success: course and time availability

The extant literature is replete with similar strategies to help ensure student success. No matter the institution, successful enrollment boils down to these ideas:

1. Be true to your mission and understand the changing demographic in order for your institution to accomplish its mission.
2. Envision what student success will look like at your institution.
3. Strategically plan the goals you will need to target to achieve student success.
4. Understand the data you need and the metrics you will need to accomplish your goals.
5. Bring together the best leaders at your institution, representing both the horizontal and vertical structure.;
6. Plan for curricular and cocurricular programming and policies to support student success.
7. Deliberatively and purposefully connect with the students, their parents, alumni, and employers.
8. Build a culture of student success where a collaborative, self-responsible ethos holds the entire community together.

The role of the Enrollment Management leader is to communicate, educate, coordinate, and plan. This helps to build a campus culture of enrollment planning, as well as the contributions necessary for every faculty and staff member in recruiting and retaining students. Campus constituents and other campus leaders will need to learn "the basics of how enrollment becomes tuition revenue . . . and of opportunities and limitations relative to financial incentives."[9]

This book has focused on the integrative and collaborative work of enrollment management and strategic enrollment planning. Curricular and cocurricular aspects are co-equal parts to the heritage of liberal arts institutions, and such integration is the only approach to make our institutions viable, even in the near-term.

In the previous chapters we scanned the terrain of institutional data and resources, the Office of the Registrar, Financial Aid, Admissions, Student Affairs, Athletics, and High Impact Practices. We pulled these strands together in this final chapter through the tapestry of strategic enrollment planning.

Still, even more focus could be given to the work of Administrative Services and its role in recruitment and retention of students. For example, tuition pricing and price sensitivity is paramount to today's students. Campus safety and beautification also play an important role. Do policies and practices help or hinder student matriculation? What is the role of Institutional Advancement in providing support to our students and in connecting alumni with them?

Even more crucial is the role of Academic Affairs. While High Impact Practices have become central features to the successful college experience, the right mix, or academic program array, must always be examined. The academic core must never be lost, but it must be contemporized to be both pragmatic and robust. Likewise, pedagogy must leave the static "sit-and-get" mentality to active intellectual engagement for the students, both within the classroom and with the local and global communities where our next generation will reside.

The work ahead seems overwhelming, but it is not. It's being done every day in your own institutions. But, alas, it is not what it could be. To take this work to the next level it will take your leadership. Your leadership to understand enrollment management and to engage with your professional staff and faculty is imperative. Your support, your guidance, and your shared role in mutual accountability is what it will take.

NOTES

1. Alexis Pope and Susan Davies. "Influencing Institutional Expectations through Organizational Leadership and Contextual Data." *Strategic Enrollment Management Quarterly,* 8(2): Summer 2020, 4.

2. Clayton Smith, Janet Hyde, Tina Falkner, and Christine Kerlin. "The Role of Organizational Change Management in Successful Strategic Enrollment Management Implementation," *Strategic Enrollment Management Quarterly,* 8(2): Summer 2020, 32.

3. Larry Shinn. "No, It's Not Just the Enrollment Crisis—It's Also Time to Modify Our Learning Paradigm," *Trusteeship:* Association of Governing Boards of Universities and Colleges. (May/June 2020), *28*(3), 20–27.

Shinn further discusses efficacious strategic thinking vs. traditional long-range planning: (24).

Strategic Thinking	Long-Range/Other Planning
• Future/Vision oriented	* Mission/status quo oriented
• Focuses on environment	* Focuses on institution
• Oriented toward change	* Oriented toward stability
• Develops integrated actions	* Develops segmented actions
• Creates synergistic outcomes	* Creates individual outcomes
GOAL: "Sustainable Distinctiveness"	GOAL: "Institutional Excellence"

4. Aaron Hanlon. "Higher Ed is Not a Zero-Sum Game: Cutthroat Competition Is Not the Way Forward." *The Chronicle of Higher Education.* June 19, 2020.

5. Ibid. Smith et al., 33. Citing the work of D. Connor. "The Characteristics of Nimble Execution. *Change Thinking Blog.* December 20, 2010. Retrieved from: <connerpartners.com/frameworks-and-processes/the-characteristics-of-nimble-execution>.

Smith and colleagues also noted many people will be critical of change and strategic planning efforts: "For example, some say too much time is spent in meetings, processes are too complicated . . . [other concerns of time and costs—staff and data systems]." 32.

6. Karen Doss Bowman. "Shifting Demographics." *Trusteeship:* Association of Governing Boards of Universities and Colleges. (March/April, 2020), *28*(2): 25.

7. *Lewis Sanborne. *Strategic Enrollment Planning: A Dynamic Collaboration* (Cedar Rapid, IA: Noel-Levitz, 2016), vii.

8. Michael Rutter. "The 8 Steps Institutions Need to Take to Improve Student Success," *Inside Higher Ed.* https://www.insidehighered.com. November 14, 2019.

Rutter concludes: "Students who succeed feel that their classes are relevant and engaging and that their professors genuinely care about their learning and their success. Active learning is valuable . . . because it engages students in their own learning."

9. Alexis Pope and Susan Davies. "Influencing Institutional Expectations through Organizational Leadership and Contextual Data." *Strategic Enrollment Management Quarterly,* 8(2): Summer 2020, 5.

Bibliography

Bahr, Steven, et al. "Stats in Brief: Why Didn't Students Complete a Free Application for Federal Student Aid (FAFSA)? A Detailed Look." US Department of Education: National Center for Education Statistcs, December. 2018. https://nces.ed.gov/pubs2018/2018061.pdf.

Berman, Michael. "New Life for Legacy Systems." *Educause Review*. Retrieved October 9, 2020, from https://er.educause.edu/articles/2019/8/new-life-for-legacy-systems.

Brynjolfsson, Erik, and Kristina Steffenson McElheran. "Data-Driven Decision Making in Action." *MIT IDE Research Brief 2017*(1). Retrieved October 9, 2020, from http://ide.mit.edu/publications/data-driven-decision-making-action.

Bustamante, Jaleesa. "College Enrollment & Student Demographic Studies." *Educationdata.org*. https://educationdata.org/college-enrollment-statistics/. July 6, 2019.

College Board, *Trends in College Pricing* https://research.collegeboard.org/trends/college-pricing/figures-tables/family-income. 2019.

Cook, Vickie. https://sites.google.com/a/uis.edu/colrs_cook/

Dale, Edgar. *Audiovisual Methods in Teaching*. New York: Dryden. 1969.

Docking, Jeffrey. *Crisis in Higher Education: A Plan to Save Small Liberal Arts Colleges in America* (East Lansing, MI: Michigan State University Press, 2015).

Doss Bowman, Karen. "Shifting Demographics." *Trusteeship:* Association of Governing Boards of Universities and Colleges (March/April, 2020), 28(2): 20–25.

Emsi. Emsi Q4 2019 Data Set. www.economicmodeling.com. 2019.

Finley, Ashley. and Tia. McNair. "Assessing Underserved Students' Engagement in High Impact Practices." Washington, DC: American Association of Colleges and Universities, 2013. https://www.aacu.org/sites/default/files/files/assessinghips/AssessingHIPS_TGGrantReport.pdf.

Grawe, Nathan. *Demographics and the Demand for Higher Education.* Baltimore, MD: Johns Hopkins University Press, 2018.

Hamilton, Laura, Josipa Roksa, and Kelly Nielsen., "Providing a 'Leg up': Parental Involvement and Opportunity Hoarding in College," *SAGE: American Sociological Association* (2018), 91(2): 111–131. Journals.sagepub.com/home/soe.

Hanlon, Aaron. "Higher Ed is Not a Zero-Sum Game: Cutthroat Competition is Not the Way Forward." Washington, DC: *The Chronicle of Higher Education.* June 19, 2020. https://www.chronicle.com/article/budget-transparency-now.

Hart Research Associates. "Key Findings from 2018 Employer Research." *Fulfilling the American Dream: Liberal Education and the Future of Work.* Washington, DC: American Association of Colleges and Universities. www.aacu.org/leap/public-opion-research.

https://www.act.org/content/dam/act/unsecured/documents

https://www.airweb.org/

https://www.economicmodeling.com/

https:///www.gallup.com/cliftonstrengths/

https://www.hanoverresearch.com/

https://nces.ed.gov/

https://nces.ed.gov/collegenavigator

https://nces.ed.gov/ipeds/about-ipeds.

https://www.princetonreview.com/college-rankings?rankings=party-schools.

https://www.ruffalonl.com/

https://www.usnews.com/best-colleges.

Kinzie, Jillian. "High Impact Practices: Promoting Participation for All Students." *Diversity & Democracy,* Washington, DC: American Association of Colleges and Universities, 15(3), (2012): 13–14.

Kuh, George. "High-Impact Practices: What They Are, Who Has Access to Them, and Why They Matter." Washington, DC: Association of American Colleges and Universities, 2008.

Lee, Peter M. "Lies, Damned Lies and Statistics." University of York. Retrieved October 9, 2020, from https://www.york.ac.uk/depts/maths/histstat/lies.htm.

Low Cost Models for Independent Colleges Consortium. www.thelcmc.org.

McCann, Adam. "Best Colleges Ranking." *WalletHub* (October 21, 2019). Retrieved October 9, 2020, from https://wallethub.com/edu/e/best-colleges-in-the-us-ranking/40748/.

McGurran, Brianna. "Students Missed Out on $2.6 Billion in Free College Money." *NerdWallet,* November 13, 2019, www.nerdwallet.com/blog/2018-fafsa-study/.

Miller, Josh. "10 Things You Need to Know about Gen Z." *HR Magazine.* SHRM.org. October 30, 2018.

NACUBO. "Before COVID-19, Private College Tuition Discount Rates Reached Record Highs," Washington, DC: National Association of College and University Business Officers. https://www.nacubo.org/Research/2020/NACUBO-Tuition-Discounting-Study. May 20, 2020.

Pope, Alexis, and Susan Davies. "Influencing Institutional Expectations through Organizational Leadership and Contextual Data." *Strategic Enrollment Management Quarterly 8*(2), Summer 2020: 3–9.

Rath, Tom. *Discover Your CliftonStrengths*. New York, NY: Gallup Press, 2007, 12.

Rhodes, Terrel. "The Changing Nature of Work and Careers," Washington, DC: Association of American Colleges & Universities, *Liberal Education, 105*(3/4), Summer/Fall 2019: 6–11.

Ruffalo Noel-Levitz. "Effective Practices for Student Success, Retention, and Completion Report," 2019. https://www.ruffalonl.com/papers-research-higher-education-fundraising/student-retention-practices-report/.

Rutter, Michael. "The 8 Steps Institutions Need to Take to Improve Student Success," *Inside Higher Ed.* https://www.insidehighered.com. November 14, 2019. https://www.insidehighered.com/blogs/higher-ed-gamma/8-steps-institutions-need-take-improve-student-success/.

Sanborne, Lewis. *Strategic Enrollment Planning: A Dynamic Collaboration* (Cedar Rapid, IA: Noel-Levitz, 2016).

Schwieger, Dana, and Christine Ladwig. "Reaching and Retaining the Next Generation: Adapting to the Expectations of Gen Z in the Classroom." *Information Systems Education Journal 16*(3) (June 2018): 45–54.

Selingo, Jeffrey. "The New Generation of Students: How Colleges can Recruit, Teach, and Serve Gen Z." Washington, DC: *The Chronicle of Higher Education.* 2018.

Shaw Brown, Genevieve. "After Gen Z, Meet Gen Alpha: What to Know about the Generation Born 2010 to Today." Interview on goodmorningamerica.com. February 17, 2020.

Shinn, Larry. "No, It's Not Just the Enrollment Crisis—It's Also Time to Modify Our Learning Paradigm," *Trusteeship:* Washington, DC: Association of Governing Boards of Universities and Colleges (May/June 2020), 28(3): 20–27.

Smith, Clayton, Janet Hyde, Tina Falkner, and Christine Kerlin. "The Role of Organizational Change Management in Successful Strategic Enrollment Management Implementation," *Strategic Enrollment Management Quarterly,* 8(2) (Summer 2020): 31–40.

Stuart, David, and Todd Nordstrom. "Are You Asking the Right Question?" *Forbes,* Forbes Magazine. Retrieved October 9, 2020, from http://www.forbes.com/sites/davidstuart/archive.

WICHE: Western Interstate Commission for Higher Education (*Knocking at the College Door.* 2016).

Wilhelm, Ian. "New Models for Assessing Applicants." *The Chronicle of Higher Education.* April 30, 2020, 1–3.

Zemsky, Robert, Susan Shaman, and Susan Campbell Baldridge. *The College Stress Test: Tracking Institutional Futures Across a Crowded Market* (Baltimore, MD: Johns Hopkins University Press, 2020).

About the Author

Perry R. Rettig has been an educator for thirty-eight years with a breadth of leadership experiences. He has written extensively on the topic of leadership and has presented his thoughts to dozens of national and international audiences. *The Quantum University* is his sixth book with Rowman & Littlefield. It examines the newer sciences and how they should impact our leadership and our organizational models. He begins by describing the classical sciences and their impact on present structures. He then describes newer lessons from the sciences and how they should impact the work of educational leaders.

After a dozen years as a teacher and as a school principal in K-12 public schools, Rettig became a professor of educational leadership and administration. The past twenty-seven years have found him in higher education serving in various capacities as a faculty member, associate vice chancellor, vice president for academic affairs, and most recently as vice president for enrollment management. He has served as a leadership fellow, and as interim deans in the school of education and the school of nursing & health sciences. Presently, Dr. Rettig serves as the vice president for enrollment management and vice president for the Athens Campus at Piedmont College in Georgia where he continues to maintain his faculty credentials.

www.ingramcontent.com/pod-product-compliance
Lightning Source LLC
Chambersburg PA
CBHW051813230426
43672CB00012B/2718